Virtuoso Teams

Michael —

Best of luck
with your
teams!

FT Prentice Hall
FINANCIAL TIMES

In an increasingly competitive world, we believe it's
quality of thinking that gives you the edge – an idea
that opens new doors, a technique that solves a
problem, or an insight that simply makes sense of it all.
The more you know, the smarter and faster you can go.

That's why we work with the best minds in business and
finance to bring cutting-edge thinking and best learning
practice to a global market.

Under a range of leading imprints, including *Financial
Times Prentice Hall*, we create world-class print
publications and electronic products bringing our
readers knowledge, skills and understanding, which can
be applied whether studying or at work.

To find out about Pearson Education publications, or tell
us about the books you'd like to find, you can visit us at
www.pearsoned.co.uk

PEARSON
Education

Virtuoso
Teams

The extraordinary stories of
extraordinary teams

Andy Boynton and Bill Fischer

 Prentice Hall
FINANCIAL TIMES

An imprint of **Pearson Education**
Harlow, England • London • New York • Boston • San Francisco • Toronto • Sydney • Singapore • Hong Kong
Tokyo • Seoul • Taipei • New Delhi • Cape Town • Madrid • Mexico City • Amsterdam • Munich • Paris • Milan

PEARSON EDUCATION LIMITED

Edinburgh Gate
Harlow CM20 2JE
Tel: +44 (0)1279 623623
Fax: +44 (0)1279 431059
Website: www.pearsoned.co.uk

First published in Great Britain in 2005
This paperback edition published in 2009

© Pearson Education Limited 2005, 2009

The rights of Andy Boynton and Bill Fischer to be identified as authors of
this work have been asserted by them in accordance with the Copyright,
Designs and Patents Act 1988.

ISBN 978-0-273-72183-3

British Library Cataloguing-in-Publication Data
A catalogue record for this book is available from the British Library

10 9 8 7 6 5 4 3
12 11

Typeset in 10pt Galliard by 30
Printed in Great Britain by Henry Ling Limited, at the Dorset Press,
Dorchester, DT1 1HD

Illustrated by Kevin Woodson

Andy wishes to dedicate this book to Jane, the love of and the rock in my life. She has allowed me to pursue my dreams. All of us Boynton boys, Owen, Dylan, Ian, Evan and myself, owe her more than can ever be put into words. She is the ultimate leader, our Amundsen, Edison, and Bernstein, all rolled into one, of our own modest virtuoso team, pursuing some great family adventures of our own through life.

For many years, Bill has wanted to dedicate to Marie at least one book for being constantly and forever the best thing that ever happened to him, and the most important part of his life. Marie: this is your book! In addition, Bill has been blessed with a great virtuoso team that has made life well worth living. The story of this team is not told in this book, but could have been. Thanks for being such a great team: Marie, Amy, Billy, Kim, Sergio, Nicolas, Isabelle and Gerome.

Thanks also to Marianne Vandenbosch for her expert help.

Contents

Authors' acknowledgements

There is a gestation period for any book and this one was particularly long and troublesome. It started quite a few years ago with the disturbing recognition that each month we'd work with yet another organization that was dedicated to attracting 'great' people into its workforce, to become the 'employer of choice' in their field, to be seen as a talent magnet on the university campuses that they recruited at, and yet, year after year, despite the continuous addition of constantly 'great' people, these same firms would return, unfailingly, *average* results. In fact, the people that we met in our classrooms and consulting engagements *were* great! They were ambitious, thoughtful, experienced, and eager to display their talent, yet they were ensnared in organizations that wasted that potential. We believe that the equation shouldn't work like this. The power of management and organization should not result in: great people in → average results out. Building organizations and adopting leadership styles that *diminish* talent instead of *aggrandizing* it is a real indictment of the managerial profession. We were sure that it didn't have to be that way. That was the birth of this project.

A few years ago, we started to search for 'success' stories: illustrations of where great talent could, under the right conditions, exceed even its own expectations. We started with all-star teams in the arts, entertainment, and science, where the experiences were much more open and accessible than in corporations where proprietary interests obscured such stories. Ultimately, we found lots of examples in the firms that we worked with, yet almost always they were reluctant to tell their stories for publication because of modesty, internal politics and even jealousy. In the end, we decided to go with what was most accessible, and vivid, and focus on a group of team experiences that everyone could learn from. These stories come from a variety of 'industries' and pursuits, but they are all about teamwork, leadership and talent, and nearly always in a competitive commercial environment.

Along the way, we had a lot of help, much too numerous to identify precisely, and we thank everyone who has been involved. A vital few, however, deserve special mention. Our families, to whom this book is dedicated, were our most ardent supporters. They provided the patience and sustenance that was essential to making this book a reality and in many instances they actually liked hearing about the stories that we were working on; but they were not alone. A whole host of managers in a variety of programs were exposed to these stories, and our arguments, as they developed, and in every instance their interest and the energy with which they reacted to this material provided us with the support we needed to turn this notion into a book. Norsk Hydro, in particular, allowed us to tell the story of their amazing success in the Bloc 34 project. Thanks very much to Knut Asebo, Jan Helge Skogen, and Torstein Dale Sjøveit. The support from IMD, the school where we both were on the faculty during the writing of most of this book was amazing. John Walsh, in particular, who was the director of R&D never lost his belief in the power of what we were doing despite some of it being a bit odd for a business school, and R&D director Petri Lehtivaara always found resources for yet another team, no matter how over budget we already were. Peter Lorange, IMD's president, was also an enthusiastic supporter of the project and added the necessary and much-appreciated 'hard shove' when we were lagging. Jim Ellert was also always supportive. Gordon Adler, who is now directing IMD's public relations efforts, was intimately involved in nearly every stage of this project, almost from the very beginning. Without him, it would have just been yet another set of interesting ideas. Valerie Noceto also provided much assistance throughout the life of the project, and we had the great privilege of working with Jackie Meyer at the start. Our colleagues were uniformly supportive and provided numerous examples of 'virtuoso teams' that they had long admired. Phil Rosenzweig, in particular, was always finding ever more obscure examples of virtuoso teams that bolstered our confidence in the phenomenon. Persita Egeli-Farmanfarma, Tanja Aenis, Lindsay McTeague, Michelle Perrinjaquet, and Jim Pulcrano were all essential contributors to this project. Their enthusiasm and the absence of competition is one of the reasons that IMD is such a great place to work.

Jaime Marshall, our first editor at Pearson, was an absolute joy to work with. He believed in the project from the moment that he learned of it and was always encouraging. His successor on the project, Laura Brundell, picked the ball up when she took the project over and never looked back. It has been great to work with them, as well as with Richard Stagg, who has overseen it all. Kirsten Sandberg, of the Harvard Business School Press, gave us essential advice early on in the project that really made a difference in what ultimately resulted. The book is much better for her insights. Robert Crawford, at the time an independent writer living in Italy, helped us develop the chapters as stand-alone business cases. This was an essential start to getting the whole project together. His writing skills can be found on nearly every page. Roland Huntford, author of *Last Place on Earth*, has become a real friend, providing us with insights that go well beyond his masterful study of Amundsen and Scott's race to the pole. Amanda Vaill, took time away from writing her forthcoming biography of Jerome Robbins: *Somewhere: A Life of Jerome Robbins*, to share her thoughts on him as a catalyst for the virtuoso team that created *West Side Story*. At IDEO, Bruce MacGregor and Dave Blakely, both suite directors, have added enormously to our appreciation of how that great organization continually establishes *virtuoso teams* as an essential part of how they do their work. Tom Stewart, Bronwyn Fryer, and Lilith Fondulas at the *Harvard Business Review*, were immensely helpful in getting us to refine our thoughts. There is a much longer list of people who we'll have to thank personally, but hopefully they'll be able to see the impact that they made on our thoughts in the pages of this book.

In closing, Bill would like to take all the credit, while leaving responsibility for any errors with Andy, and Andy believes that it should be exactly the opposite. We've both been blessed with a great partner in the other, and our own small *virtuoso team* not only made this project possible, but it was one of the great experiences in our professional and personal lives.

How to read this book

The chapters in this book illustrate the experiences of a number of virtuoso teams. The first chapter summarizes the lessons learned, while Chapters 2–8 tell the stories of each of several virtuoso teams spotlighted. These chapters can be read in any order, and it might, in fact, be worthwhile to read any one of the team chapters before reading Chapter 1. In that way, Chapter 1 will have more immediacy than merely being a general summary. Finally, Chapter 9 is about those situations where you don't have a virtuoso team, yet still want to have a higher probability of big success. In this chapter, we describe a process that we've adapted from the virtuoso teams working at IDEO, and that we've modified for managerial challenges. Each chapter ends with our conclusions and 'lessons learned.' For that reason, we have chosen not to add a separate conclusions chapter to the book.

Illustrations

Kevin Woodson, Partner, Visual Ink, LLC:

For the past 15 years, Kevin has been combining art, facilitation, and strategic thinking to create business illustrations with Fortune 500 companies, including Hewlett Packard, The Gap, and Citigroup. Kevin uses his artistic gifts to tell the story of change, make the complex simple, and get people on board and excited.

Publisher's acknowledgements

We are grateful to the following for permission to reproduce copyright material:

The Magazine of the Writers Guild of America, West for extracts from the transcript of *Caesar's Hour Revisited* broadcast on PBS 1996; and Random House Inc on behalf of Crown Publishers for extracts from *Where Have I Been?* by Sid Caesar & Bill Davidson © Sid Caesar Productions Inc. 1982.

In some instances we have been unable to trace the owners of copyright material and we would appreciate any information that would enable us to do so.

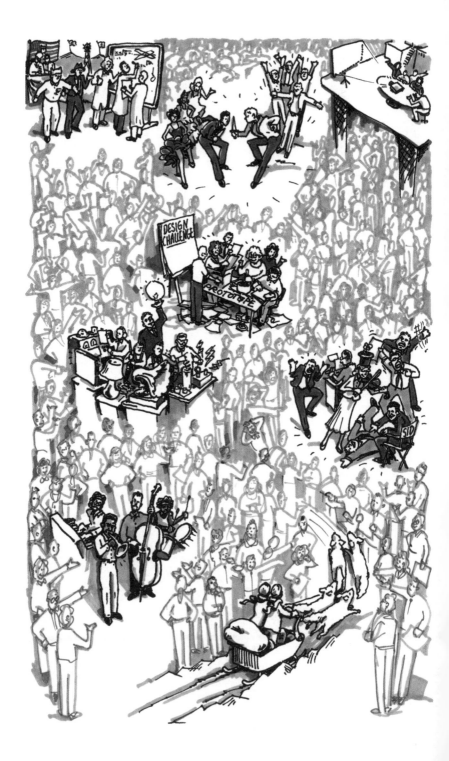

1

Unleash the talent of virtuoso teams

Managing and leading a very special kind of team

THIS IS A BOOK ABOUT EFFECTIVELY MANAGING and leading teams that are catalysts for *big change*. There are many excellent books available on how to manage teams more effectively and how teams contribute to 'high performance' organizations. These are good books and a lot of organizational improvement is built around their ideas. Our experience and research, however, suggests that *big change* is different from incremental change or 'improvement,' and that teams assembled to lead in this way need a very different approach.

When launching innovative or major new product or service lines, entering into challenging new markets, or initiating large-scale transformation of operational capabilities, virtuoso teams can make the difference between real success, or achieving just another modest result. In short, virtuoso teams offer extraordinary potential, but they need special care and handling. At the heart of the virtuoso team concept is a fundamental premise: profound change requires profoundly different management approaches. In the arts, science, athletics, business, politics, and nearly any area of human achievement, virtuoso teams offer the ultimate advantage: they put extra-ordinarily talented people together to achieve great things.

This book describes key elements to effectively managing and leading virtuoso teams. A virtuoso team is:

▌Assembled specifically for creating *big change*. Such change is radical or discontinuous change that represents a significant departure from prior practice and/or marks an abrupt departure in how an organization conducts its business.

▌Composed of individual superstars, or virtuosos, in every team position.

▌Led in a fundamentally different way from a normal team in order to unleash the absolute maximum contribution of each individual superstar.

▌A team experience that not only profoundly changes the organization, customer, or industry, but also changes the leader and team members as a career-defining moment.

▌Created specifically to be a team that does not remain together over multiple initiatives or projects. A virtuoso team has a single clear mandate associated with very high ambitions that are typically about achieving a single-minded discontinuous change.

It sounds simple, but the ingredients for virtuoso teams are rarely assembled in most organizations: they are considered 'too risky, too temperamental, too egocentric, and too difficult to control.' These are typical phrases one often hears whenever putting great talent on one team is considered. We believe, however, that if *big change* is called for, these hesitations are seriously mistaken. Time and time again, ambitious efforts led by traditional teams in organizations fall far short of the mark. Great things don't happen. Big results are not delivered. The entire organization is held back, an outcome unacceptable in today's ultra-competitive world. This is not to suggest that traditional, harmonious teams are no longer useful. Such teams continue to be essential to ensure incremental improvements and the smooth day-to-day running of many organizations. However, where *big change* is required we need to think differently.

The rules of the game are different for virtuoso teams. Keep in mind that *big change* opportunities are the most appropriate target for virtuoso teams. We've identified seven lessons essential for successful virtuoso teams and their leadership.

Seven lessons for virtuoso teams

1 Virtuoso team leaders drive the culture, vision, and action within the team context.

2 Virtuoso team leaders recruit the very best talent and never settle for what's available.

3 Virtuoso team leaders double-stretch the customer and the team to achieve ambitious goals.

4 Virtuoso team leaders spotlight the individual 'I' within the team, and not the conventional 'we.'

> **5** Organizations cultivate a marketplace for talent within the organization to facilitate the creation of virtuoso teams.
>
> **6** Virtuoso team leaders actively span boundaries and act as powerful conduits of ideas.
>
> **7** Virtuoso team leaders stimulate idea flow by managing space, processes, and time.

Virtuoso team leaders drive the action

Virtuoso teams are not democracies: they have strong leaders that powerfully drive the team, its vision, culture, and the results. Despite their emphasis on individual accomplishment and performance, all of the virtuoso teams that we've looked at have, at their center, a single strong leader. Even in situations where there are several strong individuals and occasions of shared leadership, there always emerges one individual who is the real driving force behind the team.

Such leaders drive a powerful, very ambitious vision into the fabric of their team. The visions for our virtuoso teams were typically created by one individual and ultimately shared and owned by the team. The vision holds the team together, as much for what it means to them as individual virtuoso performers as for what it means to the collective team. The vision was not negotiated, nor was it a result of compromise. The vision must be compelling enough to enlist the allegiance of those at the very forefront of their professions, who are seen as thought-leaders building the future. Almost always, the vision is bold enough to be energizing, obvious enough to be immediately attractive, yet open enough so that each star sees their place in shaping and achieving it.

The role of the 'leader' in virtuoso teams is so central to the whole story that we could have entitled this book *Leading Virtuoso Teams*. The leader sets the stage on which superb individual performance within a team context will play out. They create the whole idea for which an all-star team is needed; they select the team members. They are 'in' the team constantly – physically, spiritually, emotionally, and intellectually. It is their team in many respects. They guide, they criticize, they nourish, they reject, they test, they educate. Some of the leaders we studied had no previous leadership experience, but all of these leaders are virtuosos in their own field of expertise. They were also all smart enough to know that the stars that they hired in their particular fields of expertise knew a great deal more than they did. By virtue of their own personal brand and the attractiveness of the vision that they have, virtuoso team leaders are magnets for incredible talent.

Virtuoso team leaders dispense with unnecessary politeness that serves no purpose other than to slow the team down. After all, in the words of one of our leaders: 'Polite teams get polite results,' and no virtuoso team is interested in polite results. Leaders of virtuoso teams push the team members far beyond what they ever individually thought they could achieve. Personal relationships are strained. Tensions rise. Virtuoso teams are exhausting and contentious places to work, yet few of their members are tired when they are in the midst of such groups, and most are surprisingly energized by such an atmosphere.

Leaders engage team members in direct dialog that is frank, open, candid, and involves to-the-point conversations. This sort of dialog – versus polite, roundabout, and tepid – is a powerful source of new ideas. New ideas in turn generate richer conversations. There is also a high degree of compe-tition for ideas and the leader is intolerant of anything other than excellence. The result is that the dialog within these teams is direct and unsparing of individual feelings. You hear the leaders relentlessly criticizing performance or ideas, but not individuals. You see that the pace of dialog and the common commitment to greatness will allow individuals to give up ideas without taking it personally. The vision driving the team is the overriding objective, better and better dialog generating better and better ideas is the means to the end, not regard for personal feelings or pride.

Warren Bennis has spoken insightfully of the notion of a 'crucible' or intensely testing situation in which leaders are formed.[1] We believe that virtuoso teams serve this purpose and should be used deliberately by organizations to prepare future leadership. One of the most remarkable things about virtuoso teams is that their members almost always go on to become the leaders of their field's next generation. Virtuoso teams do not last forever. Virtuoso teams will eventually come apart as the team members follow their dreams and want to develop their individual talent to its fullest, leaving their own personal indelible mark upon the field. What is so notable about them, however, is that over and over again, virtuoso teams

1 Bennis, Warren G., Thomas, Robert J. 'Crucibles of Leadership.' *Harvard Business Review*, Vol. 80, No. 9, September 2002.

become the testing ground from which future generations of leaders are bred. Executives of smart organizations realize that the power of virtuoso teams should be leveraged by thinking of them not only as a means to increasing the probability of achieving *big changes* in the present, but also as powerful vehicles for ensuring leadership development for the future.

Virtuoso team leaders recruit the very best people

Big talent is a fundamental starting place for leaders with a vision for *big change*. Leaders who not only want to change the world, but who are actually successful in doing so, surround themselves with teams of great people. Rather than trying to do it on their own (often impossible), or having to 'pull' less capable people along with them, the leaders of virtuoso teams give themselves a head start by recruiting the best people to help them achieve their goal.

Recruiting more talent, rather than less, results in more ideas, more energy, more creativity, and higher performance. This may seem obvious, but it's definitely not the norm. For many traditional team efforts, members are chosen for the wrong reasons. They might be good team players, or available with no present assignments, or have a certain personality that may fit into the desired team concept, or need an opportunity to work on a project or to learn other functional areas. Many reasons exist: but the result is a team of some combination of interesting, nice, available, motivated, and skilled professionals. Talent is factored in, of course, but it's just one of several considerations. No wonder that success is problematical. This is not the case with virtuoso teams. With laser-like focus, virtuoso leaders zero in on recruiting extraordinary talent and resist 'dumbing down the team' or moving the talent bandwidth towards 'average' by over-considering any other criteria than ones that will get them to achieve the team's big vision for change.

Recruiting great talent is strategic because creating a revolution is not for the faint-hearted and certainly not for the modestly talented. Any time you talk about 'revolution,' you must acknowledge that there are major gaps to be bridged between the present and the future; between what may be and what is; between our talents and our dreams; and between what we want to accomplish and who we presently are; and what we are presently capable of achieving. Confronting and overcoming such gaps is a demanding experience. Unfortunately, the gap between where we want to be and where we are is often narrowed the wrong way. The gap is not going to be closed by compromising on the vision or composing a team of mediocre or even 'good' performers. Rather than less ambition or a team condemned to modest results, virtuoso teams offer another starting place. Recruiting the very best talent and unleashing them in a virtuoso team is a place to start reaching our highest ambitions. Establish the right team to make an exciting vision happen, don't lower the ambition for where your organization wants to be.

Ironically, an obsession for great talent is not the norm when creating traditional teams. Instead, all too often, ambitious leaders who sincerely want to change the world are almost immediately placed at a significant disadvantage because they don't seek out and recruit the very best people. Instead, they settle for those who are on hand, or for whoever's available. Frequently, they also misinterpret the popular wisdom about 'teamwork' and create or tolerate teams that might be harmonious in their team's culture but are, as a result, almost inevitably preordained to produce another round of mediocre outcomes.

How do leaders attract virtuoso talent? After all, they have an abundance of alternative opportunities. Unlike leaders who rely on others in the firm to find team members, leaders of virtuoso teams first put themselves in a position where they know who these people are – in their business unit, their organization, their industry, or even in their profession – and then they go out and get them. This is not by chance. They take the time and make it their responsibility not only to keep up with business, but also to keep up with talent. The leader makes it their job to spend time reading, scanning, networking and searching: identifying, listing, and meeting the best talent inside and outside the organization. Each of the teams that we'll look at was explicitly composed of the best people obtainable. The team leader did this personally. This presents a very different approach from a leader merely accepting or choosing from the 'best people available.'

Contemporary 'wisdom' regarding teams and talent typically emphasizes 'hire for attitude, train for skills.' We believe that this results in teams with great attitudes, but insufficient skills to change the world. On the basis of our studies, we would argue that when *big change* is desired, managers are well advised to 'hire for skills and attitude be damned.' Virtuoso teams succeed with all-stars because of what they know, not because of how agreeable they are.

In almost all of the cases, the virtuoso team leader had a strong personal brand and was a 'magnet for talent.' Individual virtuoso performers would seek them out for a chance to work with them, and would never think to decline such an opportunity. Working with these leaders was seen as 'the place to be,' and such 'fame' was well known throughout the community of interest. Typically, this was often a result of the leader's own individual virtuoso reputation, as well as reflecting that they were well known for giving others a chance to express their talent, reach their potential, build their professional capital, and build their careers.

Virtuoso team leaders break the rules to recruit the people that they feel are essential to the team's success. This may require that they get people from outside of the organization, from other projects, fight over the objections of others in the organization, or reward all-star performers. In each of these virtuoso team cases, the leader is involved with the selection of the people on the team, knows why they are there, and, in fact, wants them specifically – by name and reputation – because of some specific talent that they bring to the team. The team members know this and, consequently, assume the attitude of an elite. We believe that this attitude is a critical early step towards assuring team success.

If you want to change the world, or your piece of it, we believe that you should deliberately stack the odds in your favor. Recruit the best virtuoso talent, and then create a team environment that respects this talent and tries to unleash it, rather than constrains or diminishes it.

Virtuoso team leaders 'double stretch': they stretch the team and the customer beyond what either imagined

Virtuoso team leaders challenge their teams not only to stretch themselves to heights of greater intensity and effort, but also to stretch the customer's experience by delivering unanticipated and higher levels of fulfillment. This double stretch energizes the team and reinforces the self-confidence that is the hallmark of the individual star-performer within a powerful team context.

Virtuoso team leaders set 'stretch' expectations by letting everybody inside and outside the team know that this team will drive profound change forward and go well beyond what is typically accepted as 'high performance.' By setting clear expectations, leaders of virtuoso teams give the team an explicit challenge: unleash your extraordinary talent to create *big change*, or fail in everyone's eyes. From their first moment of engagement, each team member knows they are there to do something great and that people outside the team have the same expectations. We believe that this initial stretch plays an important role in preparing the virtuoso teams we studied to ignite the full potential of their individual and collective talents. As Katzenbach and Smith found in *The Wisdom of Teams*: '[a] demanding performance challenge tends to create a team.'[2] We believe that a stretching challenge for an all-star team is essential to produce exceptional individual and team performance.

Stretch targets ignite competitive instincts of virtuoso performers. The combination of identification as an 'all-star,' and then being assembled with other 'all-stars' to tackle a major challenge, has an energizing effect on talented individuals. In a sense they're being given a chance to really show what they are capable of achieving, and furthermore they're being given the unusual opportunity to do it with teammates who are as good as they are. Inevitably, this provides real motivation to excel.

Stretching the customer completes the double stretch concept that is a feature of virtuoso teams. *Big change* cannot be accomplished unless the customer or the target audience is also changed in some way. Virtuoso team leaders and their members believe that the customer wants more, not less. Virtuoso teams think about the customer in an 'ennobling' rather than in a diminishing fashion, and are not misled by prevailing views of what the customer wants. They believe that their customer is better than they've typically been stereotyped as, and then they deliver against that higher perception. This is not suggesting merely pushing more products, services, or solutions to the customer. Rather, the virtuoso team delivers to the higher vision that they have of the customer. The team believes that the customer is far more complex and interesting than they are typically given credit for being. Virtuoso teams avoid 'stereotyping,' as

2 Katzenbach, Jon R., Smith, Douglas K. *The Wisdom of Teams: Creating the High-Performance Organization*. New York: Harper Business, 2003.

that almost always leads to diminished, rather than enlarged, visions of the customer. They give the customer credit for being capable of demanding and appreciating *big change*, and then let the customer help them achieve such change.

This double stretch – the internal challenge within the team and the enrichment of the ultimate customer/'stakeholder'/'user' experience – is contrary to what we see so often in teams that exist in organizations where average results are acceptable. These teams typically have views of their customers that are frequently uncharitable, or may even be derisive or contemptuous. The perception is important, for the product that they deliver to the customer ultimately reflects this view. Not surprisingly, the customer in turn frequently conforms to the assumptions. It becomes a self-fulfilling prophecy. Everyone is satisfied with a mediocre status quo. Until, that is, some competitor comes along and delights the customer with what they have to offer. New customer expectations emerge and some competitors are left in the dust. In our research on virtuoso teams, displeasure with the 'mediocre' status quo was often the breeding ground for the virtuoso team emerging to change the rules of the game.

Nearly all of the teams that we'll see in this book have created the possibility for their members to stretch themselves in ways that often exceeded what they imagined possible. In addition, this is almost always done in an explicit effort to stretch the customer, who then has typically responded with tangible appreciation in terms of enthusiasm, revenues, resources, and support.

Virtuoso team leaders spotlight the 'I,' not the 'we'

The virtuoso leaders we studied enabled each 'I' –
individual star performer – to soar, allowing great talent to
produce even greater results without becoming
preoccupied with the 'we' that influences so much
contemporary management thought. Rather than fitting
individuals into behavior that emphasizes – 'we' –
teamwork, virtuoso teams leaders refuse to diminish the
power of the individual 'I.' They deliberately constructed
their teams around the individual superstars that they had
attracted. They emphasized the individual 'I's' rather than
the collective 'we's' of the team. Extraordinary talent is
about the 'I.' It has to be set free and allowed to perform
solo in order to achieve its full measure. Why get great
talent on the team, and then average it down to keep
everyone happy? Virtuoso teams are not about getting
polite results.

We think a pivotal problem facing many organizations
today lies in the contradiction between individual talent
recruited, and the team performances achieved.
Organizations that we typically see pride themselves on
hiring 'great people.' Leaders boast about their workforce,
profile them in annual reports, and aspire to be amongst the
preferred employers on university campuses. These
organizations spend time building recruiting processes that
give them an edge in identifying great talent and, in some
cases, even resort to hiring bonuses. Organizations typically
strive to out-recruit their competitors. The result is a lot of
good people entering these organizations, year after year,

but the rather average financial and market results that these same firms return, year after year, suggest that this highly sought-after talent is diminished by the organization, rather than aggrandized. Somehow, the addition of premium talent has no effect. How can this be? This is an indictment of everything that we believe in as the power of organization and leadership. We believe that the answer lies in the way that the high-performing individual is regarded in too many modern organizational contexts.

Organizations hire 'great people' because they are great at what they do as individuals. The achievements of these people that make them attractive in the first place are individual achievements. Almost always, they've performed within groups or organizations, but it is as individuals that they have vividly stood out. Then we bring them into 'our' organization and all too often we constrain the very elements that made them attractive in the first place. Teams succumb to the same problems. Talent is diminished. Underachievement is the norm.

The organizational contexts that constrain individual talent include barriers created by title or function, credentials, or experiences; a preoccupation with following the rules versus insistence on getting great results; a culture that encourages convergence of thinking rather then accepts divergence; and perhaps a sense of 'we' that permeates the organization and provokes mistrust or dislike for anyone who dares to stand up and proclaim 'I.' Barriers create an 'iron cage' that restricts individual talent. Individual talent is squandered, potential lost, and promise unfulfilled. The latest yearly

HR survey may indicate that the workforce is satisfied, but the results in the market are uninspiring. The survey also masks an important fact – the most talented individuals are typically the most frustrated. All of this is a real indictment of leadership. The power of organization and leadership should be to fulfill individual promise, not deny it. Great leadership is about taking talented 'I's' and doing extraordinary things, not about taking good talent and doing mediocre things.

Leaders of virtuoso teams break through organizational inertia by building around individual talent and designing a context that sets it free and lets it reach its full potential. Leaders start with the potential of the individual superstar and then construct the team around letting talent(s) soar, rather than the other way around. A team of 'I's' is not a team that looks for consensus or expects harmony in the way in which it works. Almost inevitably, these are teams of big egos and strongly-held opinions. Tension becomes a way of life in virtuoso teams, rather than being something to be avoided or minimized. In these teams, this tension is regarded as an asset to team performance. Virtuoso teams are not only aware of these tensions but embrace and manage them, rather than seek to avoid or deflect them.

One of the lessons that come out of our examples is: never shy away from creating élites when *big change* is required. Get the best people that you can, even if it means going well outside of your group to do so. Settling for whoever is available, or for the people that happen to be on your team already, is a distinct willingness to start off a project with a serious handicap. Endorsing pure meritocracy as the basis for high-profile team recruiting may not be 'politically correct,' but it works in terms of improving your chances for actually achieving *big change*. Allowing all-star high-performers to be recognized as such should be a positive thing, not a negative one. While this has a bit of a Darwinian edge to it, we believe that competition and challenge are invigorating factors.

Virtuoso team leaders draft from a 'marketplace' for talent in their organization

Mobility of talent is a hallmark of organizations where virtuoso team leaders thrive and succeed because they draft the very best people they can get. We refer to such conditions as being a 'marketplace for talent,' where fluidity and movement of talent must be allowed. When we look at why so many organizations that pride themselves on hiring the best people consistently deliver average results, we can't escape the conclusion that one of the reasons for the non-fulfillment of promise is the lack of freedom that leaders and talented individuals have: freedom to build their own or join teams, set their own goals, determine their own future, set their own course, or establish their own pace and cadence.

Leaders of virtuoso teams not only identify great talent, they go out and attract that talent to their team. In large organizations, getting the best people possible on the right team means that traditional ways of allocating talent – often done by some central HR function – is at odds with the needs of the team and the vision of the leader. What we've seen in the virtuoso teams that we've looked at is that some sort of mechanism to allow, if not encourage, fluidity in talent acquisition is important.

In a very real sense, anyone in an organization who is an all-star performer should be fair game for virtuoso team selection, no matter where they were formerly located. If the stakes are high, why construct barriers to join the very best team that is working on blockbuster projects? The mobility of talent is important for getting the right talent onto the right team. This may require considerable imagination as to what the idea of easy mobility within an organization should really mean. Trying to really emulate an actual market for talent allocation is not something that is instinctively welcomed in large organizations. What a marketplace for talent really does, however, is to return the power of career determination to the individual, with the release of all of the enthusiasm and energy and commitment that that entails.

Projects are central to an effective marketplace for talent. Great talent wants to be associated with great projects and great leaders. Our view is that almost regardless of the industry chosen, projects are becoming increasingly important to competitive advantage, organizational learning, talent development, and getting things done.

Many organizations today embody two fundamental types of work. Progress is achieved through projects driving change and initiatives. Everything else is heading for processes – replication, scale, measurable, improvable, reuse of know-how. Computers, routines, procedures are the heart of processes. They are important, but often it is not where the fun is. Projects allow 'end to end' ownership and opportunity to entrepreneurs.

Teams drive projects and this is where individual talent rises to the top. Getting in the way of talent finding the right project and reaching its full potential strikes us as self-defeating, especially for organizations and leaders with big ambitions that need teams driving radical change of some sort. And, when talent is mobile, the leaders are put under pressure to build a reputation for creativity that they nurture, develop, and unleash. Virtuoso team leaders have to 'attract' team members.

Projects become more than simply 'jobs' or challenges. They become much more socially complex and represent the results of a market between project, leader, and potential team member. Although the project may be a great idea, for example, a dysfunctional leader won't be able to attract talent because their team is not an attractive place for high-performers to be. Great projects and great leaders become seen as opportunities for growth and advancement. Ambitious talent wants to get onto the 'tough' assignments and work with the best leaders. They understand that the more they risk, the more they may possibly gain.

Virtuoso team leaders span boundaries, becoming conduits for great ideas

Virtuoso team leaders define themselves by the area of their professional expertise. We suspect they typically don't define themselves as 'leaders' in a traditional sense, yet they fulfill much of what we look for in great leaders – energy, edge, engagement, and vision. Incredibly they also earn respect for their creative and professional expertise.

Successful virtuoso team leaders expand the boundary of their expertise by spanning the inside and outside of the team for new ideas. Effective boundary spanning means leaders must effectively be on the prowl for great thoughts and be a conduit for new ideas flowing into the team dynamics. Boundary spanning and being a conduit for ideas doesn't just happen. It takes hard work and lots of practice. Virtuoso team leaders spend time getting smarter each day. Rather than meandering through a day or week and hoping they stumble on a few interesting ideas that they might take back to the team or organization, leaders must consider how they become better boundary spanners and conduits for great ideas.

The best virtuoso team leaders actively plan and manage:

1 how and where and when they acquire talent and ideas, and;

2 how to put them into play within the organization.

Both sides of the equation are needed, the acquisition of great ideas and putting them into play. We all know leaders or managers who have great ideas and yet when they articulate those thoughts, they are dead on arrival. We also know leaders or managers who are great at articulating ideas, but never have anything really interesting to say to push the organization forward. Both situations are unacceptable for leaders of virtuoso teams. Too little attention has been given to this simple yet critically important notion – that leadership is an idea-intensive profession that has to be taken seriously.

TABLE 1.1 Virtuoso team leaders vs. other team leaders

What virtuoso team leaders do	What many team leaders do
Is obsessed with new ideas; is always on the prowl listening for the next 'edge'	Ideas are subordinate to 'real work,' has no conscious sense of where he gets his ideas from; it's mostly hit or miss. Typically relies on traditional sources
Recognizes that assembling the best people obtainable, field-by-field, and putting them into direct, challenging dialog, increases the likelihood of getting a great idea	Accepts the best people *available*, and then encourages conviviality
Has a vivid and compelling vision of big change that acts as a magnet for leveraging the ambitions of others	Accepts the project as given, and assembles a team around it
Is a consummate professional dedicated to the advancement and personal learning within her field of expertise	Works within a field of expertise to earn a living and sells his time
Has a broad and varied appreciation for a wide range of interests, all of which are drawn upon to build better insights into her field of expertise	No connection between external and professional interests; lives on two planets
Shares what she reads and learns with colleagues; creates an environment where everybody is always learning	Never thinks to communicate new ideas to others; is frequently too focused on the job at hand

What virtuoso team leaders do	What many team leaders do
Takes an active interest in the work of others; plays a central role – physically and professionally – in all aspects of the team's activities	Is narrowly focused on his own work; can't spare the time to be interested in the work of others; is frequently absent, or remote
Is not afraid of confrontation within the group, as long as it leads to higher performance	Insists on harmony within the group; will sacrifice ideas to reduce conflict
Holds the customer or target market in high-esteem; is inspired to 'stretch' the customer	Views the customer through unflattering stereotypes; assumes that they want less, not more
Manipulates time and space deliberately – to generate new ideas	Is oblivious of the power of time and space in generating new ideas
Sets the parameters for the team and then gets out of the way	'Directs' all activity, instructs each team member out in the exercise of their expertise
Attracts great individual talent and then builds team around the talents' promise	Assembles talent in a way that is always subordinate to the team's objectives

Virtuoso teams are arenas for the powerful idea flow that produces the sparks of creativity, innovation, and emotion which are catalysts to radical change. Ideas are the basic building blocks of creativity, innovation, and accomplishment. Great things start with great ideas. The leaders of virtuoso teams are often the authors or co-authors of new ideas that mark a significant departure from the way that others think. We've discussed how virtuoso team leaders assemble the best talent possible in order to have the best ideas possible. That is just a start in building a team into an idea engine. Virtuoso team leaders take steps to make sure those ideas are put into play by insisting on intense dialog, debate, and argument. Virtuoso team leaders, and members, cherish new ideas and the spontaneous creativity and energy that occurs when ideas collide. Such leaders instinctively know that it is not the 'stock' of knowledge that counts, but rather the 'flow' of ideas. Idea flow is managed carefully and with energy. Idea flow between talented people triggers even bigger ideas and possibilities. This idea flow is where spontaneous connections are made. This is one foundation of successful radical change. It can't just be more of the same. Great ideas that are executed are what virtuoso teams are all about. Great ideas don't just happen, however, and leaders of virtuoso teams understand that these connections are not spontaneous, nor do they occur by pure chance.

Virtuoso team leaders stimulate idea flow: managing space, time, and processes

In virtuoso teams, leaders do more than span boundaries as a conduit for great ideas. That's important, but the attention to ideas does not stop with their personal behavior. We have found that leaders stimulate idea flow as a source of team advantage. To get ideas moving, they pull several levers that they have at their disposal; the physical space, processes, and time.

Virtuoso teams draw strength from the intensity and closeness of the work. Ideas, feelings, and actions become a cauldron of excitement. Energy is created and not diminished, as is so often the case in traditional team meetings. Attention to the pace and space are essential ingredients to high-performing virtuoso teams. Personal space becomes subordinated to the need for team intimacy. Overcrowding and chaos become the catalyst for cracking barriers between team members and turbo-charging great conversations. When virtuoso teams are in action, the conversation and dialog become the critical units of achievement, not the work itself. Conversation and direct dialog are the mechanics by which ideas move and radical change takes off. Virtuoso teams nurture this dialog. They create the space where it can, and in fact must, occur.

Taking team members out of their comfort zones, physically, is a key to moving them into their collective creativity zone. To lead a virtuoso team is an exercise in the choreography of idea flow, bringing together space, time, and talent to create a breakthrough.

Virtuoso teams thrive on experimentation through prototyping. Insisting on a fast-paced style of 'idea testing and learning,' virtuoso teams create prototype after prototype in order to test ideas that are new, bold and daring. Virtuoso team leaders also recognize that prototypes are a 'work in process' and that the only way to really move the team forward is to try a lot of new things and see what works and what doesn't. Failure is a source of learning, not something to be avoided. Virtuoso team leaders are impatient to create change and they push to test ideas through prototyping sooner rather than later.

Why squander exceptional talent on ideas that won't work? Not only does prototyping ideas result in rapid learning, prototyping also embodies an essential tool for managing risk. If ideas are prototyped frequently and tested with customers, then the final prototype is far less likely to be way off the mark. Prototyping keeps the focus of the team on what really works, and what doesn't. These teams frequently border on chaos. They operate at a pace that is many times the speed of normal teams, they work in close physical intimacy and have direct dialog without unnecessary politeness. They are exploring unknown frontiers, and have extraordinary self-confidence. In such situations, prototyping becomes a natural part of how a team works. It becomes part of the culture and the attitude. Be bold and provocative, try it, and learn. It's the way great ideas are generated and connected.

Leadership is a contact sport in virtuoso teams. Whether it's recruiting new talent, moving ideas back and forth, designing the next prototype or facing the customer, leaders of virtuoso teams position themselves right in the middle of the action. Without this direct 'hands-on' intimacy – both physical and emotional – there is no way that virtuoso teams can be effective. They are full of competition and they are full of conflict as talented individuals vie with each other to get their ideas across. The leader of the virtuoso team needs to be in the middle of all of this, adjusting the pace, making decisions, consoling those whose ideas do not prevail and maintaining the energy, if the team is to fulfill its promise. This cannot be done 'remotely.' In a very real sense, the 'brand' of the virtuoso team is the brand of the leader, so their immediate presence and involvement is absolutely essential.

The virtuoso teams in this book

We believe that we can learn from great teams that are all around us. No matter what business we are in or what workplace we are a part of, there are lessons in leadership that are observable in the experiences of more visible organizations that are also struggling to change their situations. Profound change is about ambition and execution. Profound change is about leadership. It doesn't matter if we're talking music, or science, entertainment, or exploration, we must learn from the experiences of others. In fact, since teams that work within the fields of music, science, entertainment, and exploration are often so much more publicly visible than teams that work within the organizational and proprietary confines of traditional commercial organizations, by opening our eyes to the organizational and leadership experiences of these teams we add to our archive of lessons and insights about our own situations. Accordingly, this book seeks out leadership lessons from a wide variety of organizational experiences, including:

> Leonard Bernstein and his collaborators who launched a revolution on Broadway with the introduction of serious music, classical ballet and social consciousness, simultaneously, in the award-winning, commercial blockbuster *West Side Story*. Despite a high-risk idea that didn't rely on a happy ending, and repeated rejections by the venture capitalists who fund Broadway theater, the all-star team, which also included Jerome Robbins, Stephen Sondheim and Arthur Laurents, overcame numerous hurdles to fundamentally change the way we think about contemporary theater.

Up against some of the stiffest scientific competition ever assembled, and with the security of the 'free world' at stake, the scientists assembled for the Manhattan Project not only created the atomic bomb, but ushered in a whole new world of managing 'big science' that has continued to the present.

Light (electric incandescent), action ('talking' motion pictures), sound (recorded sound)! All are the product of an unlikely team of seriously smart people who were called 'The Muckers,' by their leader, Thomas Edison. Despite the fact that his team worked together more than 100 years ago, they launched several major technological revolutions that not only changed their world but also remain important parts of ours as well and their message is still very relevant today.

Roald Amundsen's expedition team, the first to make it to the South Pole, in 1911. This team was up against stiff competition from the much better-resourced, much larger, and bigger-branded English expedition party of Robert Falcon Scott but Amundsen's team was handpicked so that he had an 'all-star' player at each position. Their success was extraordinary despite their constraints, and they set the standards for exploring the unknown in many different fields.

The birth of television in the early 1950s also created the challenge of developing new content for the new medium. Sid Caesar, a comic genius, surrounded himself with a virtuoso team of other geniuses, including Woody Allen, Mel Brooks, Carl Reiner and Neil Simon, and created a commercial success that dominated the industry in its early days.

Miles Davis and the reinvention of jazz in the 1940s, 50s, and 60s. Three times, Miles Davis assembled all-star bands (entirely different teams for each decade) in successful revolutionary efforts that completely redefined the existing jazz world of the time. The results were: 'cool' jazz, 'modal' music, and 'fusion.' Each of which was both an artistic and a commercial breakthrough.

Norsk Hydro, the giant Norwegian global energy player, had to recover from a strategic crisis and applied their very top professionals to address a major surprise in their global oil exploration efforts. Hydro's leadership had the wisdom to put aside traditional bureaucratic responses to the situation, and they assembled a virtuoso team that moved super fast to dampen an impending disaster.

Each of these teams embraced *big change*. Each of these teams had real commercial objectives and constraints to work within. Each of these teams was in a tough business, with serious competitors striving to beat them. And, each of these teams succeeded! Such examples provide a new perspective on how great teams achieve great change.

How to use this book

Over the next seven chapters you will have the opportunity to visit a number of fascinating virtuoso teams up close. Don't be skeptical of their suitability for you simply because they come out of a different culture to yours, individually or organizationally. Treat every experience as an opportunity to learn. Each of these teams took on the odds, were ambitious, hired the best people and got more out of them than even the individuals thought were possible, and in most cases not only successfully achieved their revolution but established the basis for future leadership as well. We'll comment throughout on what they are doing and why we think that it's important, and we'll return to a more specific summary at the end. In the final chapter we'll propose a systematic approach for turbo-charging teams in your organization to achieve near virtuoso-like performance. This approach can be used across a wide variety of projects and initiatives as a way to jump-start the teams you unleash to create the future of your organization.

At the conclusion of each chapter we'll provide a set of questions for you to ask about how you, your leaders, or your organization are, or are not, using virtuoso teams. The questions are intended to get you to reflect on the key points about managing or leading virtuoso teams that appear in each chapter. Each question is augmented by a short discussion of where the chapter spotlighted the particular issues we are asking you to think about. Asking the right questions can often lead to the deepest insights, and we urge you to think about these questions yourself and with your colleagues in your efforts to use virtuoso teams to lead the *big changes* that your organization faces.

Virtuoso leaders recruit the best and then allow them to be as good as they can possibly be. The following successes are not by chance, but result from conscious, energizing leadership of teams of outstanding individuals. This is somewhat different from the traditional 'team concept' which is typically represented by a collective portrait in which harmony reigns and everyone is smiling. *Big change* requires a fundamentally different view of what teams are and how they work.

From these lessons there emerge a few questions that you should answer when launching your next virtuoso team:

1 When big change is the goal, do you truly insist on doing everything possible to assemble the best talent obtainable, no matter where it is located? Or do you instead use the people available, even when you know that they are not the best possible?

2 Is it possible for your organization to provide sufficient internal mobility so that the best talent can be called upon when needed, even by other departments or functions?

3 Do you strive to preserve individual excellence within a team context? Do you let the 'I's' surface, or overly obsess about the 'we's'?

4 Do you take great individual talent and somehow diminish it to a group average in the way in which you establish team behavioral norms? Or, do you let the expertise truly rise and let consensus and democracy fall by the wayside at times?

5 Do you establish the overall parameters that you desire for your people, and then let them get on with figuring out how to achieve these? Or, do you not only set the goals, but also tell others how to achieve them, in a way that destroys the enthusiasm and creativity of your people?

6 Do you listen, really listen, to your team members?

7 Do your teams easily identify great new ideas, and then move them through the organization rapidly? How effective are your team's conversations? Are your conversations direct ones? Is everyone engaged in the conversation? Are the best ideas coming to the surface and are your teams grabbing them, and making them happen?

2
Stretch the customer, stretch ourselves

The impolite team behind West Side Story

Why did Lenny have to write an opera, Arthur a play, me a ballet? Why couldn't we, in aspiration, try to bring our deepest talents together to the commercial theatre? That was the true gesture of the show.[1]

Jerome Robbins in the 1950s

West Side Story has been one of the most successful and enduring musicals to ever appear on Broadway. It was the product of an extraordinary team of virtuosos, who threw themselves into a high-risk, exhausting collaboration which resulted in great artistic and commercial triumph. Essential to the success of this particular virtuoso team was their willingness to reject contemporary stereotypes of their customers, and to give them more than was typically thought they were prepared to accept. In doing this, to stretch their customers, they also pushed themselves to new artistic heights. We call this 'double stretch' and it is a key characteristic of the virtuoso teams that we see in this book. Double stretch is about getting the most out of your team and making the biggest change possible, for both you and the customer. With double stretch in place, the stakes are high for success, or failure, and *West Side Story* illustrates how true, belly-to-belly collaboration in virtuoso teams is driven

1 Garebian, Keith. *The Making of West Side Story*. Ontario: Mosaic Press, 1995.

by direct, open dialog and an intense focus on the outcome, not on maintaining polite relationships in the team. The collaboration is fostered by intense intimacy, earmarked by tight emotional bonds and close physical proximity.

The creation of *West Side Story* also illustrates another powerful lesson for those embarking on virtuoso teams to change their world: there is no room for compromise – the words 'good enough' are the first steps towards a mediocre result. 'No compromise' might mean not sparing personal feelings or being willing to bruise a few egos along the way, but if the best people are assembled and committed to create big change, then there is an obligation to take advantage of the opportunity and to make the most of that talent. This is, indeed, the legacy of West Side Story. The venture was a huge commercial success, with the subsequent movie winning several Oscars and the music continuing to reach listeners everywhere. This is the story of the team that turned Broadway's conventional form on its head and created *West Side Story*.

The birth of an idea that stretches both the virtuosos and the customer

East Side Story, the saga of Jews and Italian Catholics engaged in a Passover rumble, never made it beyond the conceptual stage, but from this kernel of an idea, with a little help from William Shakespeare's *Romeo and Juliet* and a great virtuoso team, was born a cross-town successor that changed the face of American theater and resulted in the creation of one of the most enduring pieces of popular music created in the modern era: *West Side Story*. The original idea for *West Side Story* belonged to one of the brightest talents in the world of dance in New York City in the middle of the 20th century – Jerome Robbins, a young ballet choreographer.

Robbins had been intrigued by the prospects of a
contemporary social commentary, based on the elements
found in *Romeo and Juliet*, for some time. On January 6,
1949, Robbins telephoned a young composer-conductor,
Leonard Bernstein, to ask if he would be willing to
collaborate on a contemporary version of *Romeo and
Juliet* for Broadway, to be set in New York City. The show
would be a gang-warfare drama between Catholics and
Jews on the East Side of Manhattan. It would be called
East Side Story. Would he be willing to hash out the
concept at his apartment along with Arthur Laurents,
whom Robbins wanted as librettist? Robbins had chosen
Laurents on the basis of the book *Home of the Brave*,
which he said had him '. . . [crying] like a baby.'[2] The
story would be, in Bernstein's words, 'a tragic musical-
comedy [that could change] the face of American musical
theater.' Not only would it incorporate a social theme with
a noble purpose, it would integrate song, dance and drama
rather than highlighting only one genre as was the custom
on Broadway. All of this would be new to an American
Broadway production. For each of the principals, this was
a major artistic departure from previous work. At critical
junctures in the evolution of their careers, each was
suddenly considering a venture that would take them
away from the safe path. Each was warned off by mentors,
yet each was also intrigued by the opportunity to change
the way that America was entertained. Was this a big
personal risk for all? Absolutely. But it was also a huge
opportunity as well.

2 Lawrence, Greg. *Dancing With Demons*. New York: Berkley Books, 2001,
p. 232.

The birth of a virtuoso team: a vision to change Broadway

During the 1950s, Broadway musicals were limited by a number of self-imposed conventions: the shows tended to blend nostalgia, comedy, and feel-good endings. It was easily marketable entertainment, a formula for 'popular' stars. Tragedy, social critique, and even 'art' had little occasion to bloom in that context. In addition, the various genres of entertainment – dancing, singing, and acting – tended to be separated rather than integrated. A typical hit of the day was *My Fair Lady*, a light-hearted, song-based comedy that required little acting or dancing. Then along came a number of rebels, including Jerome Robbins, who wished to extend the potential of the Broadway musical.

The project was the idea of Jerome Robbins, who had had prior success with several imaginative dance productions, including the ballet hit *Fancy Free* and the subsequent movie which was based on it, *On the Town*. He was a deliberate, ruminative type of thinker, not at all impulsive, who kept a tenacious grip on a stream of ideas which would, over time, yield one great success after another. Once he had an idea, he never gave up and, since he had a lot of ideas, and a compulsive work ethic, he was destined to become a serial innovator in the world of dance and entertainment. He was driven in a quest for perfection in everything that he did. As one of the cast in this show put it:

> He really made an art of keeping people on their toes by demanding that they work as hard as he did. He'd say, 'I'm working hard. I want you to work hard too. I want this to be the best thing you've ever done!'[3]

3 Ibid., p. 77.

The *Romeo and Juliet* theme was one of the ideas that Robbins clung to throughout his career, and several earlier efforts had employed the theme in a variety of situations. Robbins also had prior experience working with groups of virtuosos, although perhaps not *virtuoso teams*: creating and choreographing the dance program in the Broadway musical *Miss Liberty*, for example, was the creation of a team of virtuosos, including: music by Irving Berlin, direction by Moss Hart, based on a book by Pulitzer Prize-winning author Robert Sherwood, and with sets by Oliver Smith. It turned out to be a flop, however, which prompted the observation that it was the story of 'how five geniuses can make one turkey.'[4]

In January 1949, Robbins, Bernstein, and Laurents met together as the *East Side Story* team for the first time: 'I remember that evening in Jerry's apartment as though it were yesterday,' Bernstein recalled, 'because of the excitement.' Almost immediately, however, the idea ran into trouble. Although intrigued by the project, Laurents – a budding playwright and Hollywood scriptwriter in his own right – did not want to play a subordinate role to Bernstein. 'I want to make one thing clear before we go any further . . . [Laurents screamed] I'm not writing any f***ing libretto for any goddamned Bernstein opera!'[5] While Bernstein did his best to smooth things over, another observer quipped: 'You'll never write it . . . three temperaments in one room, and the walls will come down.'[6] The egos were huge and so was the talent. Coexistence as one team loomed as a major challenge from the start.

4 Ibid., p. 145.
5 Zadan, Craig. *Sondheim & Co.* New York: Harper & Row, 1974, p. 14.
6 Garebian, op. cit.

There were many other obstacles which appeared insurmountable, as well. In part, because of the tragic theme, several top producers felt the project to be very high risk and had already turned Robbins down. The team was hard-pressed to find funding to even begin. In addition, the team members were all too busy to throw everything aside and work on this project. As a rising classical music star, Bernstein was already badly over-committed and would be unavailable for long periods of time. Moreover, Bernstein's mentor, the European conductor Serge Koussevitsky, was openly scornful of 'low class' Broadway musicals and pressured him to stick to the classics. As a result, not only was the reputation of Robbins on the line with this radical concept, but so too was Bernstein's career. Finally, Bernstein and Laurents sensed that the concept was stale: 'gang warfare' between Jews and Catholics on the East Side was a thing of the past. Bernstein decided to pursue other projects and the idea was shelved.

The vision stays alive and opportunity strikes

Six years later, a chance meeting reignited the project. While in Hollywood to write the musical score for Elia Kazan's *On the Waterfront*, in 1955, Bernstein ran into Laurents at the Beverly Hills Hotel pool. Laurents was there to work on a screenplay. Inadvertently, the two of them noticed a newspaper headline about gang fights between Mexicans and Americans. As Bernstein recalled, 'Arthur and I looked at one another . . . [and] suddenly it all [sprang] to life. We could feel the music and see the movement. It was electric. We could visualize the future product.'[7] Then, why not, Bernstein asked, do it about a Puerto Rican gang? They were frequently in the news in New York and there was much talk of conflict with 'Americans.' When they returned to Manhattan, they contacted Robbins with the revised idea. Robbins became convinced that the idea could work now; and this time set on the West Side of Manhattan.

The team quickly began to build momentum, though it lacked a lyricist and producer. Robbins was immediately brought back into the idea and in Bernstein's words: 'A second solemn pact has been sworn. Here we go. God bless us!'[8]

Enter Sondheim: great talent is a magnet for great talent

A lyricist was needed to provide the words, and a young protégé of the great composer Oscar Hammerstein, Stephen Sondheim, became the newest member of the core *West Side Story* team.

Hammerstein had taught him the utter necessity of simplicity, how to introduce character, make songs relate to character, how to tell a story, and the interrelationship between lyric and music.[9] When Laurents bumped into Sondheim at a party, he remembered having heard him sing at an audition for another show, and invited him to play for Bernstein, who recounted:

7 Zadan, op. cit., p. 15.
8 Lawrence, op. cit., p. 232.
9 Zadan, op. cit., p. 111.

> I went wild . . . I thought he was a real, honest-to-God talent. The music didn't sound terribly distinguished – it sounded like anybody's music – but the lyrics didn't sound like anyone's lyrics by any means.[10]

Although Sondheim was brought into the team by Arthur Laurents, both Robbins and Bernstein were well known for their talent and creative material-searching proclivities. Robbins once observed: 'I had a very special eye out looking for material . . . The 'eye' becomes a sort of Geiger counter which starts to tick in the brain and emotions as you approach a subject of value to you.'[11] The trio immediately offered Sondheim the job of collaborator on lyrics, in effect sharing the credit with Bernstein. Though his career was stalled at the time, Sondheim initially felt reluctant to join the effort. Not only did he consider himself first and foremost a composer, but he also felt humiliated and embarrassed to be a mere 'collaborator' on lyrics. In the end, it was Hammerstein who convinced him to sign on. Once Sondheim had joined the core team, the four collaborators had intense conversations and debate and finally forged a vision by agreeing on what they did *not* want. Said Laurents:

> Neither formal poetry nor flat reportage; neither opera nor split-level musical comedy numbers; neither zippered-in ballets nor characterless dance routines. We didn't want newsreel acting, blue jean costumes or garbage-can scenery any more than we wanted soapbox pounding for our theme of young love destroyed by a violent world of prejudice.[12]

10 Garebian, op. cit., p. 36.
11 Lawrence, op. cit., p. 186.
12 Garebian, op. cit., p. 39.

Moreover, Bernstein wanted to achieve something totally new and different, risky and breathtaking in scope. He pushed the team to create the crudest of outlines, which was an effective prototype that accelerated the play in a way that gave form and precision to the delicate balance between 'opera and Broadway,' between 'realism and poetry,'[13] and allowed them to worry about the final conceptualization at a later stage. Sondheim also met another prerequisite for joining the team: a willingness to work hard. While Jerry Robbins was well known for spotting talent, it was also quite apparent that he could recognize 'ego' in others, and that he had no patience for anyone who was not totally committed to the work. Sondheim met the test on both accounts. In the case of Bernstein, with whom Robbins had collaborated several times in the past, and who was world-renowned for his ego, Robbins respected Bernstein's total work commitment and could ignore the ego as a result.[14]

Getting big resources and big support: the matter of a producer

A suitable producer proved extremely difficult to find, which stalled the project even further. From the many producers who were approached and declined came the word that the concept was too violent, too angry and, with two bodies on stage at the end, simply too unpleasant for Broadway. For the time being, the team found only one solid financial backer, Roger Stevens, who was dedicated

13 *Leonard Bernstein: Reaching for the Note*, 1998. Video. USA: Educational Broadcasting Corporation.
14 This example comes from Vaill, Amanda. *Somewhere: A Life of Jerome Robbins*. Forthcoming publication.

but who insisted that other investors join as well. When they finally signed on the seasoned producer Cheryl Crawford, who was widely recognized for her theater work during the Great Depression, she brought great moral authority to the project.

To their dismay, however, the collaborators soon discovered that Crawford was playing them one against the other in an attempt to gain control. An extremely important developmental milestone was reached when, in the face of her demand that the libretto be changed to be more to her liking, the four principals – hardly a team at that point – silently rose as one, and left her office in silence. This saw them without a leading producer, but it forged them into a real team. Nonetheless, with only six weeks before rehearsals were set to begin, it appeared that everything would fall apart.

At this low point, Crawford's partner Roger Stevens' commitment to the project and the team helped the collaborators to push ahead. They then telephoned Harold Prince, a producer and friend of Sondheim who had already turned down the idea. This time, Prince joined the team; he was attracted to unconventional and surprising material, willing to put promising unknowns into starring roles, and able to balance business and artistic criteria. By joining their production, Prince went against the advice of his mentor, the director George Abbott, who disapproved of this 'gang musical.' Thus, with this project, he struck out on his own, which was a risky career move. With Prince's enthusiasm, funds to cover the entire production were quickly raised.

The all-stars blend their talents: script and design

With the core team in place and the work beginning, tensions ran high. Robbins was everywhere, cajoling, figuring out what was on everyone's mind, opening lines of communication between the core collaborators, and, when need be, imposing his will. An additional trio – also of first-rate talent – was hired to design lighting, costumes, and scenery. At Robbins' instigation, everyone on the team worked closely, often blurring their roles in spite of their job titles and specialties.

By Robbins' design, the collaborators' efforts closely overlapped. As conceiver, choreographer and director, Robbins pushed his colleagues to understand what the others were trying to do. With characteristic bluntness, he constantly questioned and challenged them. For example, upon hearing the song 'Maria' for the first time, Robbins screamed at Sondheim, 'You mean, [Tony] just stands looking at the audience? What is he doing?'[15] In his way, Robbins induced Sondheim to 'stage it.' He needed to better engage the audience with the action that should take place during his song. It was typical of the manner in which the roles of the core collaborators merged. Each felt they contributed vital elements to the production as a whole. Robbins related:

> Arthur would come in with a scene, the others would say they could do a song on this material, I'd supply, 'How about if we did this as a dance?' . . . The essence of it was

15 Garebian, op. cit., p. 121.

that we gave to each other, took from each other, yielded to each other, surrendered, reworked, put back together again.[16]

These intimate interactions continued through all phases of the production, with changes, additions, and cuts, until the very end. A spirit of mutual support slowly developed, with Robbins at the center as the grumpy and demanding catalyst. For example, toward the end of rehearsals, Bernstein and Sondheim realized that the character Tony needed clearer delineation early on. When they looked at the libretto, the words: 'Something's coming' seemed to leap off the page for them. In the space of a single day, they wrote a new song to fill the gap.[17] Said Bernstein:

> I remember all collaborations with Jerry in terms of one tactile feeling: his hands on my shoulders . . . I can feel him standing behind me saying, 'Four more beats there,' or 'No, that's too many,' or 'Yeah – that's it.'[18]

Bernstein worked in the same way with Sondheim, sometimes separately, other times writing in the same room. When they hit an impasse, they played games together for hours. Yet, when any or all of the writing team met together again, they were willing to rework everything to satisfy the instincts of one another. In 1990, after Bernstein's death, Robbins looked back at their collaboration on *West Side Story*, and reflected:

> 'The continual flow between us was an enormous excitement.' [19]

16 Garebian, op. cit., p. 116.
17 Garebian, op. cit., p. 120.
18 Garebian, op. cit., p. 119.
19 Lawrence, op. cit., p. 248.

Robbins' assistant director, Gerald Freedman, thought that:

> '. . . these guys were so career-driven – but nobody
> thought it was going to be a hit. They weren't working for
> a hit . . . it was only about excellence . . . So there was a
> wonderful commitment to the work.'[20]

A conduit for ideas: actively seeking experiences to enrich the product

The team knew they had to create a realistic and powerful
experience, mirroring the emotion and tension found in
the streets of New York. Bernstein composed the score of
West Side Story to bring out the underlying themes and
crystallize emotion. The music was fresh and new, but
powerful and timeless. It was beautiful and has lasted for
five decades as both an amazing artistic statement and as
one of the most commercially successful collaborations of
our time. But the music was not enough by itself. To make
this work, there needed to be a story and action and
movement as well.

Every physical movement in the first act was designed by
Robbins to dramatize the themes of power-seeking and
doomed love. At the end of the first act, in 'The Rumble,'
dance took the place of song, with the killing of Riff and
then Bernardo, and portrayed all in action (violent dance)
and music (metallic, dissonant, and somber). The second
act opened with two comic numbers that doubled as
cynical social satire; it then moved into the longer dances,
'Ballet Sequence,' 'Taunting Scene,' and 'Finale.' Although
these dances expressed the theme of impending tragedy,

20 Lawrence, op. cit., p. 249.

they also portrayed the opportunity for love to conquer hate. At the end, sitting over her murdered lover, a sobbing Maria cannot complete her song, which the orchestra takes over from her.

To make this totally realistic and to make sure they were working with ideas vividly representing the 'real thing,' Robbins ventured into New York's neighborhoods to learn first hand and observe youth gangs directly. In a festival in Manhattan's Little Italy, he witnessed a possible rumble in the making. 'It was frightening,' he recalled. 'You could feel the tension so thick . . . I sneaked up behind a knot of the kids and listened to them calmly discussing whether they could settle whatever the argument was by a fair fight.'[21] He also observed youth gym dances; providing him 'the sense,' he said, 'of containing their own world. Not arrogance, exactly, but a crazy kind of confidence. And there was always a sense of tension.'[22] The ideas he picked up in the streets of New York went directly into the dance scenes he was imagining, which he would complete once he had his cast on hand.

Selecting the best talent and casting Tony and Maria

With the script nearing completion, Robbins had to put together the appropriate cast, get them to perform in accordance with the collaborators' evolving vision, and continue to mold the production as it developed.

21 Garebian, op. cit., p. 117.
22 Garebian, op. cit., p. 118.

Finding the right cast presented innumerable challenges: they had to be able to dance, sing, and act as young and authentic ethnic characters in equal measure. Traditional stars probably would not do; they were too specialized. In addition, seasoned professionals and stars were often too old and refined for the youthful roles in the production. According to Bernstein, they wanted 'forty kids . . . who never sang [much] before. Anything that sounded more professional would sound more experienced, and then the kid quality would be gone.'[23]

For the early auditions, Robbins even brought in amateurs and working-class youth, but the mix of required skills proved too demanding. Instead, Robbins and his team sought fresh professional talents, including newcomers, stunt men and even a former marine, who knew how to wield a knife and hence could aid Robbins to accurately choreograph 'The Rumble.'

The principal stars, Tony and Maria, were found in two young actors: Larry Kert and Carol Lawrence. After numerous audition appearances in which she was paired with Kert, Lawrence asked if they could study the script together and return later; this created expectations of a polished, high-quality performance at their next audition. 'It was a risk,' according to Kert, 'People tend to be more lenient when actors have the music in their hands, but Carol decided to go for broke and we worked on 'Tonight' for three or four days.'[24] However, when they arrived at the studio, Robbins turned the tables on them. Rather than

23 *Leonard Bernstein: Reaching for the Note*, 1998. Video. USA: Educational Broadcasting Corporation.
24 Garebian, op. cit., p. 110.

simply listening to them, he ordered Kert to wait offstage. To Lawrence he then said: 'You, Maria. See that scaffolding . . . find out how to get up there. Then stay there, out of sight.'[25] When he entered, Kert was instructed to find Lawrence, then figure out how to get to her, all of which injected tension and urgency into their performance. At the end of their song, Bernstein walked up and said: 'I don't know what's going to happen. We have more people we promised to hear. But that is the most mesmerizing audition I have ever seen.' As Lawrence began to cry from the stress, Prince added, 'No, really, you're Maria!'[26] They were offered the parts later that evening.

Stretching the performers

Robbins demanded a full eight weeks to rehearse, which at the time was far longer than Broadway convention. According to Prince:

> He is gun shy. He hates to go into rehearsal. He's the fellow standing on the edge of a precipice; you, the producer, have to push him over (which naturally makes you responsible if the show fails!). But when he finally goes, of course, it's galvanic.[27]

As a *Method* director, Robbins sought to develop the cast members' portrayal of individual personalities. At first, he posted articles on the walls about interracial gang warfare and encouraged others to find and share similar articles. To push them further, not only was each gang member given a name and biography – for the first time on

25 Garebian, op. cit., p. 110.
26 Garebian, op. cit., p. 111.
27 Lawrence, op. cit., p. 161 and 339.

Broadway, there was to be no anonymous chorus – but they were also forbidden to use any other names in the theater. Robbins then segregated the cast into their respective gangs and forced them to eat together as well as arrive and depart together; this sparked genuine group antagonism. 'This stage is the only piece of territory you really own in this theater,' he told them. 'Nothing else belongs to you. You've got to fight for it.'[28] He subjected the cast to extreme pressure. The character 'Anybody's,' who was a homely teenager excluded from the Jets, was forced to live out the alienation of her character, eating alone and rarely fraternizing with the cast.

Finally, Robbins continually posed questions to the cast about their characters. He went beyond the contents of the simple biographies that they were supplied, such as what their parents were like. 'I want my dancers, just as in acting, to find an emotional justification for . . . whatever they're doing,' he explained. 'I want them to understand who they are and what they are.'[29]

Stretching each other

Each of the four principals in this virtuoso team had already established a track record for hard work, but it is no exaggeration to suggest that the *West Side Story* collaboration pushed them to work harder than they ever had before. One observer of this scene has suggested that it was, 'the very team that allowed them to try the things that pushed the project forward. Great collaboration creates

28 Garebian, op. cit., p. 112.
29 Garebian, op. cit., p. 119.

great competition. You feel pressured to 'top' your collaborators.'[30] An example of this is the role of Oliver Smith, arguably the fifth member of the virtuoso team. Smith was a set designer of considerable talent and renown, who first worked with Robbins and Bernstein designing the sets for *Fancy Free*, and later *On the Town*. When *West Side Story* really began to take on life as a project, Jerry Robbins wanted Smith, specifically, for the designs. Smith joined the team and immediately recognized that this was truly a once-in-a-lifetime collaboration and delivered a set suggestion that was like nothing the team had thought of before. Unlike traditional stage designs which would have as many as four sectors of the stage separated by valences or draperies, Smith elected to create '. . . a fluid, cinematic kind of scene-shifting – [which] had never been done in a Broadway musical . . . [In response], Jerry [Robbins] found his ideas about staging being stretched to accommodate Oliver's scenic concept: it was no longer enough to allow actors to come on- and offstage, they had to move with the scenery, as if they and the set units were part of a complex ballet.'[31] In the give and take between Smith and the team, each side continued to up the ante around what the set would ultimately look like, each side pushing the other to be more daring. Smith challenged Robbins to make the set more cinematic and less 'booky,' and Robbins came back to challenge Smith to go even further. In the end, the repartee between Smith and the others over the set design is a vivid representation of the, 'sense of adventure which is the whole gesture of the show.'[32]

30 Vaill, Amanda. Private communication, August 2004.
31 Garebian, op. cit.
32 Vaill, op. cit., August 2004.

Relentless perfectionism

Robbins' style was as demanding as it was abrasive. As a total perfectionist, Robbins drove his cast as hard as he drove himself, taking advantage of their youth and inexperience to place brutally frank demands on them. Members of the cast frequently broke down in tears before his unpredictable abuse. 'The slightest mistake in a dance step, gesture or word met a fate worse than death,' Lawrence remembered. 'Almost daily, Jerry would single out someone for criticism – for the entire day!'[33] According to Kert: 'If you come on stage and don't give him exactly what he's pictured the night before . . . he destroys you. People thought we were puppets on strings.'[34] It is not surprising that one former co-worker observed that 'I'm not afraid of Hell when I die, because I've worked with Jerry Robbins.'[35] Yet at the same time actor Jack Klugman spoke of Jerry as: '. . . the only genius I've ever worked with, the only one. If he told me to jump out of a window, I would do it, and it would be good.'[36] Virtually nothing, it seemed, would stop or soften him. For example, while rehearsing the scene where Tony tells Maria that he killed her brother, Lawrence was instructed to beat Kert's chest in rage as hard as she could. They spent hours repeating this scene. Finally, when a doctor examined Kert for excruciating chest pains, he warned the actor that the blows might separate his lungs from his ribcage. As Robbins was informed that the chest punching

33 Garebian, op. cit., p. 112.
34 Garebian, op. cit., p. 111.
35 Lawrence, op. cit.
36 Lawrence, op. cit., p. 272.

had to stop, he retorted: 'Hit him in the head – you can't do any damage there.'[37] Another time, Lawrence fell stomach-first to the floor after a leap; as she stood up in great pain, Robbins ordered her to leap again – this time, he added sarcastically, with the 'Maria catchers' *ready*.[38]

Nonetheless, Robbins was getting the cast to achieve things beyond what they imagined possible. According to Lawrence:

> It was his modus operandi to berate and belittle us into anger so we would prove him wrong by jumping higher or turning faster or hitting each other harder in a fight sequence. He drove us to fear or hate him – sometimes both. But the result permitted us to experience a potential in ourselves that we would otherwise never have known existed.[39]

Set designer Oliver Smith characterized Robbins in the following way: 'He lives by his work. His work is Jerry Robbins. It may seem ruthless, but it isn't because that's what he's about. He is more involved in his work than in his human relationships.'[40]

Moreover, as the dancers experimented with their ranges, Robbins was inspired by them, as well. 'I am influenced by the dancers,' he acknowledged, 'I see how they move, and this stimulates my own creative thinking.'[41] As such, Robbins left many parts of the choreography open to the interpretation of the dancers, allowing them to improvise to an extent while on stage.

37 Garebian, op. cit., p. 113.
38 Garebian, op. cit., p. 113.
39 Garebian, op. cit., p. 114.
40 Lawrence, op. cit., p. 85.
41 Garebian, op. cit., p. 119.

The whole experience was incredibly demanding for all involved. Carol Lawrence [Maria] recalls that the four principals seemingly worked around the clock. Bernstein, in his diaries, confesses to being exhausted, but also admits: 'this play has become my baby. . . [which] might turn out to be something special.' The disagreements were endless, but in the end, Bernstein recalls that: 'it was a very easy collaboration . . . it was as if the four of us were writing the same script.'[42]

Testing ideas

A hallmark of Jerry Robbins' work was the ability to select talent and then make the most of it. This involved often reworking the ideas or concepts to best utilize the talent that he had attracted, which in turn meant that a Robbins' production inevitably meant a lot of experimentation. *West Side Story* was no exception. To marry experimentation with learning, Robbins adopted the approach of having several alternative 'versions' [prototypes] for each dance variation. He would then experiment with various versions before deciding on the version to go to market with; and, in the case of *West Side Story*, still revising on opening night.

Divergent leadership: contrasting styles

In contra-distinction to Robbins' 'bad cop' persona, Bernstein and Prince formed a 'good cop' counterpoint for the cast. From the sidelines, they had observed Robbins'

42 *Leonard Bernstein: Reaching for the Note*, 1998. Video. USA: Educational Broadcasting Corporation.

style with discomfort. Prince, who later went on to become a director himself, realized then that he had to be liked by collaborators in order to work. Although he recognized that the competitive atmosphere was energizing for some cast members, Prince hated the turmoil and tension that Robbins created. Bernstein took a more sensitive and nurturing approach, consoling cast members who had received the Robbins treatment and even changing the score to eliminate parts that made them uncomfortable or were beyond their natural range. 'He would work for us on an individual basis for hours, and we couldn't take our eyes off his face,' Lawrence recalled, '[because] so many emotions were written there. He never lost his temper or his good manners. He didn't drive us; he led us by believing in us.'[43]

Robbins' relentlessly demanding style of leading was by far the most controversial, and was so throughout his career. Dancer Joan Tewkesbury, who appeared in Robbins' *Peter Pan*, put it succinctly:

> 'He was a tremendous influence on me, shithead that he was . . . He was hideous . . . but it really gets down to if you can't stand the heat, get out of the kitchen. As sick as it sounds, I would have gone back to that kitchen every opportunity I had, because every time I went back to it there was one more piece of fuel that would fuel me as an artist to create.'[44]

Chita Rivera, who starred in the movie version of *West Side Story*, offers the perspective that:

> '. . . if [Robbins] hadn't been the way he was, none of those people would have danced the way they did. None of them

43 Garebian, op. cit., p. 115.
44 Lawrence, op. cit., p. 228–229.

would have had the careers that they had, as far as I'm concerned, because people give up, we all give up, and we give up a lot of times too soon . . . he made you do what you were really capable of doing, something you never even dreamed you could possibly do, he made you do . . . '[45]

Bringing it to market: finishing touches

The first tryout performances in Washington, DC were a success with audiences. Nonetheless, a number of items required last-minute changes. To modify the score on one occasion, Robbins pulled the conductor aside and simply deleted the notes he did not want. Neither consulted nor amused, Bernstein walked out of the theater to a nearby bar, where Sondheim found him with, 'three scotches lined up before him.' Artistic recognition was also an issue. Because Sondheim's name did not appear in the first news-paper articles about the production, Bernstein gave up all credit for the lyrics as well as the royalties; he even removed his credit as lyricist from the official score, which meant it had to be republished. Finally, to guard the artistic integrity of the work, they ignored a threat to picket the work on account of its references to Puerto Rico as an, 'island of tropical diseases.' In spite of these and other changes, the work kept its unity and seamless balance of dance, acting, music and text.

Eventually, although the show received mixed critical reviews, it did well at the box office. After more than 760 performances on Broadway, it went on a national tour before triumphing around the world. In a 1960 Broadway

---

45 Lawrence, op. cit., p. 255.

reopening, the critics were far more uniform in their praise, which helped to ensure that it became one of the world's most popular musical dramas. It also became a hit film in 1961, dominating the Oscars for that year, as well as a best-selling popular recording. As the first truly integrated dance-musical, it was a creative breakthrough that set a new standard for future Broadway productions. Moreover, it enabled other creative teams to address subjects even more controversial than gang warfare in later years. In fact, the team around *West Side Story*, rose to leadership in many of their individual fields, leaving Alan Johnson, a Shark understudy who rose to become one of Jerry Robbins' trusted assistants, to refer to the experience as the 'University of *West Side Story*.'

Implications for leading virtuoso teams: Summary and Key Questions

The team that created *West Side Story* did not just settle on giving the market what it wanted. To be more precise, they thought more of the customer, rather than less. At a time when the customer was stereotyped as being mindless, the *West Side Story* team anticipated social changes and stretched the customer to appreciate a new and richer form of entertainment.

It was a risk, but it paid huge dividends. If you have a virtuoso team energized to change the world with a new product or service value proposition, make sure that this team is not delivering the same as you or competitors have delivered before. That's a waste of talent and effort. Aim their sights higher to a potentially new and richer value proposition that changes how the game is played. Make sure that they are seeing the customer in a new light, not what they've assumed will be accepted. What would really make a difference in their lives or in their businesses? Stretch the customer and consider using the best talent to create something new and novel that might *really* delight the end user.

The four virtuosos that created *West Side Story* debated and argued and fashioned the detailed nuances of their final vision, almost from the very moment that they met. In doing so, they stretched themselves – this is what 'double stretch' is all about. By clearly articulating what they did 'not want,' each team member knew the rules of the game.

The direct dialog allowed for a mutual appreciation and understanding that enabled them to blend their diverse talents to change the face of Broadway. The intense discussion and open idea exchange was of equal if not greater importance than the ultimate vision itself. The team owned the vision. It wasn't superimposed. It is at this point where buy-in and commitment will achieve results, a necessary early step in the life of a virtuoso team. Your all-star teams should collectively create their own vision for the future. They must be fully engaged in no-holds-barred, direct dialog that will allow them to appreciate each other's talent to effectively blend those abilities once the work begins. They must really own their vision, rather than it being superimposed by some corporate interest.

The *West Side Story* collaborators did far more than 'work together.' The spirit of their effort was true collaboration. They freely gave each other advice and offered opinions beyond their own narrow specializations. They welcomed opportunities to be challenged by the other team members in the pursuit of perfection. They worked in close quarters, elbow-to-elbow, in an effort to energize each other throughout the duration of the intense production process. Such collaboration is much richer than traditional teamwork where professionals still cling to their specializations, and don't step on each other's toes. Collaboration, in the spirit of West Side Story is how your most talented teams should blend their talents in pursuit of the most compelling and important overall vision.

From idea generation, to selling, to production, to final delivery, these are the steps taken by the *West Side Story* team quartet. The energy and power that this creates and the ability to weave an idea into a final cohesive product or service is far more preferable to individuals working somewhat isolated, at their own pace and not in synchronization, where an idea limps its way to the market. From the very moment of inception, the *West Side Story* principals making the key decisions knew that they'd have to live with them in the marketplace, and this drove their energy and commitment, as well as their risk-taking behavior.

It has been said that the *West Side Story* team worked so closely together that they 'cooked' as a team. The ideas flowed from one to another. It was hard to see who actually created what. Many of the ideas, however, came from outside of the team. Robbins' patrolling of the streets of New York City listening to gangs embarking on a rumble or attending dances throughout the West Side, for example, resulted in powerful ideas infiltrating the thoughts and dialog within this virtuoso team. He knew that there were ideas he had to bring from outside the team, to inside the team. This is true with your team as well. There are more ideas outside of it, than in it. That's a fact. Getting those ideas in is one of the leader's key responsibilities.

A few words about leadership are important here. We don't believe that *West Side Story* would have ever become the revolution that it was without the uncompromising role that Jerome Robbins played. This role was essential to the outcome. He was more committed to the excellence of the project outcome than being liked. We think that there is a place for such a demanding leadership role in virtuoso teams. Perhaps Bernstein's role as a moderator and reconciler was a natural compliment to Robbins' hard-driving style? The point is that together this team went well beyond the sum of their individual talents and changed the world as a result.

From these lessons emerge a few questions that you should answer when launching your next virtuoso team:

1 Is your virtuoso team doing a double stretch? Are they stretching their own abilities and, as importantly, stretching the customer to appreciate new standards of excellence and making the implicit explicit?

2 Is your virtuoso team intimately involved in a direct dialog and having an open exchange of ideas to sharpen the vision they will own and pursue?

3 Is your virtuoso team engaged in true collaboration: physically, emotionally, and intellectually connected in pursuit of their vision?

4 Does your virtuoso team have an opportunity to go from the inception of the idea through to its final delivery to the customer, end-to-end?

5 Are you, or the leader of your virtuoso team, scanning for ideas and acting as a conduit, bringing those ideas back into the team?

6 Is the leadership of your virtuoso team demanding non-compromised excellence?

References

This chapter was based on a number of very useful sources:

Bernstein, Leonard. *The Joy of Music.* New York: Simon & Schuster, 1963

Garebian, Keith. *The Making of West Side Story.* Ontario: Mosaic Press, 1995

Gordon, Joanne. *Art Isn't Easy: The Theater of Stephen Sondheim.* New York: Da Capo, 1992

Lawrence, Greg. *Dancing With Demons.* New York: Berkley Books, 2001

Jovitt, Deborah. *Jerome Robbins: His Life, His Theater, His Dance.* New York: Simon & Schuster, 2004

Laurents, Arthur. *West Side Story.* Radnor: Chilton, 1973

Lawrence, Carol. *Carol Lawrence: The Backstage Story.* New York: McGraw, 1990

Vaill, Amanda. *Somewhere: A Life of Jerome Robbins.* Forthcoming publication.

3

The critical ingredients for critical mass

Using time pressure to trigger talent in the Manhattan Project

It was the late 1930s and the Nazi menace was goose-stepping its way across Europe occupying, one after another, capital cities of the 'old world': Copenhagen, Oslo, Amsterdam, Brussels, and Paris. Nightly, Nazi bombers struck at the last bastion of freedom in a devastated Europe: an increasingly isolated London. As Americans watched in horror, many felt that it was only a matter of time before US forces would be called on to defend their own homeland, time appeared to be running out and matters were grim. Then, came word to the Allies that even though the situation was bad, it could very likely become even worse. The Nazis were actively pursuing the very secrets of the universe itself in an effort to develop the ultimate weapon: an atomic bomb. Intelligence indicating that Hitler was seeking an atomic bomb stunned Western leaders, lighting a hot fire under ongoing policy discussions on the potential of atomic warfare. In addition, Hitler's Operation Barbarossa, a massive attack on the Soviet Union that began in June 1941, appeared to be raising the stakes in Germany's quest for eventual world dominance. At about the same time, American physicist Ernest O. Lawrence drew attention to a new man-made element, plutonium, which could supply enough atomic fuel to create a bomb before the end of the war,[1] but it was a monumental task to turn this into a military weapon, and it would require a large team of the best brains available in a race against time. Clearly, if there was ever the need for a 'virtuoso team,' this was it.

The Manhattan Project was America's answer to the Nazi challenge. It was both a top priority military program and perhaps the most ambitious scientific project ever undertaken. In addition to the scientific and engineering challenges, it was also, at that point, the largest industrial undertaking of all time. And it represented a virtuoso team on a grand scale: arguably the assemblage of the largest group of all-star scientific talent in the history of mankind. In October 1939,[2] US President Franklin Delano Roosevelt officially created the American attempt to build the atomic bomb. No effort should be spared; go get the brightest and the best. Unsaid, of course, was that along with all this talent would come opinions, egos and some of the most individualistic people ever to be put into a team context. It was obvious to all that it would be necessary to find leaders who could get the most from such a talented but challenging team, in a situation where success or failure might make the difference between the free world's victory or defeat.[3]

The Manhattan Project assembled a team of unprecedented brainpower – some of the most brilliant scientists of the 20th century – to design and test the first atomic bomb. Operating under enormous time pressure, they created the first large-scale practical application of the new 'nuclear' physics and the most powerful weapon ever. Sharing leadership responsibility, Leslie Groves and J. Robert Oppenheimer forged a unified and coherent team from scores of scientific superstars, with no single

1 Kevles, Daniel J. *The Physicists: The History of a Scientific Community in Modern America.* New York: Knopf, 1977, p. 325.
2 Rhodes, Richard. *The Making of the Atomic Bomb.* New York: Simon & Schuster, 1995, pp. 303–15.
3 Ibid., pp. 367–69.

person claiming credit or ownership of the ideas that went into it. In this chapter, we'll see how Groves and Oppenheimer organized this project so as to get the most out of the talent that they had assembled. We'll also see how they handled the bitter controversies that erupted between such exceptional, yet extremely stubborn and self-centered individuals. We'll learn how they kept ideas flowing and alternative options alive when a policy of 'compartmentalization' was introduced to reinforce boundaries, and reduce the ever-present security threat. In short, we'll see quite a few lessons that most managers could benefit from when approaching *big change*.

Leslie Groves: the first of two pivotal leaders

The Manhattan project was, first and foremost, a military project, and America's top military leaders decided that 46-year-old, Army engineer Colonel Leslie Groves had the unique combination of leadership qualities for the job: he was able to find and organize talent, he was an experienced project manager, and he was very tough. Having just overseen the building of the Pentagon, which as the world's largest office building at the time was also one of America's most challenging physical projects, Groves was given 'total authority' over the entire Manhattan Project, which was to become one of history's most challenging intellectual endeavors. Groves' mandate for leadership included freedom from congressional inquiry for the duration of the war, and would eventually involve 600,000 people, with as many as 160,000 employed at any one time.[4] He was not

---

4 Norris, Robert S. *Racing for the Bomb: General Leslie R. Groves, The Manhattan Project's Indispensable Man.* South Royalton Vermont: Steerforth Press, 2002, pp. 227–28.

the first choice for this project, however. His short-tenured predecessor in running what ultimately became the Manhattan Project, was removed because of a lack of urgency and indecisiveness, two traits never associated with then- Colonel Groves.[5]

Groves was a career Army officer and graduate of West Point, with an engineering degree from MIT. He was known as being both extremely capable and extremely difficult; he was a tireless worker, utterly devoted to the task at hand, and he was endowed with ruthless confidence. While 'disliked' by many of his colleagues as arrogant and utterly indifferent to the impression he gave others, he was nonetheless also respected as a man who could get things done.[6] According to one colleague, Groves was: 'the biggest sonovabitch I've ever met in my life . . . He had an ego second to none [but] you never had to worry about decisions being made or what it meant.'[7] Groves realized that this once-in-a-lifetime opportunity was accompanied by unprecedented personal and professional risk. On one occasion, he reflected that:

> If our gadget proves to be a dud, I and all of the principal Army officers on the project ... will spend the rest of our lives so far back in a Fort Leavenworth dungeon that they'll have to pipe sunlight into us.[8]

5 Ibid., p. 172.
6 Rhodes, op. cit., pp. 424–26.
7 As cited in Rhodes, op. cit., p. 426.
8 Norris, op. cit., p. 175.

In spite of his authoritarian streak, Groves preferred to
encourage his subordinates to experiment and compete,
which allowed mistakes and multiple paths to be
explored. He sought decisive workers who were unafraid
to take risks and deplored endless debates on options.[9]
To manage his superstar teams, Groves followed a number
of precepts:

1. recruit the best;

2. delegate as much as possible, avoiding direct control of
   every detail;

3. transform existing departments and offices into
   vehicles for the purpose rather than create needless
   bureaucratic duplication.[10]

The result, according to at least one observer of the project
was that he became, 'the indepensable person in the
building of the atomic bomb'[11]:

> The Manhattan Project did not just happen. It was put
> together and run in a certain way: Groves's way.[12]

Concerned about working with so many academics – 'the
greatest bunch of prima donnas ever seen,'[13] as he
described them – Groves knew that he had to find a
scientist of unimpeachable quality to act as laboratory chief,
a technical leader whose breadth of vision would pull
everything together.[14] In other words, he needed a

9 Rhodes, op. cit., p. 431.
10 Norris, op. cit., pp. 192–93.
11 Norris, op. cit., p. x.
12 Ibid.
13 As cited in Kevles, op. cit., p. 331.
14 Rhodes, op. cit., p. 425.

knowledge worker with passion for the project. For his part, Groves could handle the politics and military bureaucracy. He and the lab chief would function as co-heads in each of their domains. At a luncheon in October 1942, Groves was immediately taken with physicist J. Robert Oppenheimer, whom he came to believe was a genius.[15]

A second leader found: a remarkable young American physicist – J. Robert Oppenheimer

Along with Ernest Lawrence, during the 1930s, J. Robert Oppenheimer had built a world-class physics department at the University of California, Berkeley. However, his reputation there was checkered. When Oppenheimer chose to charm, there were few who could equal him. He could show himself to be extremely sensitive to the feelings of everyone present, anticipating their needs and wishes. His breadth of knowledge ranged from theoretical physics to poetry and Sanskrit, which both dazzled and intimidated his colleagues. However, he could also be abrasive and arrogant, dismissing those who could not keep up with his lightning-quick reasoning.[16] Concerned with the war, at the age of 38, he became a leader in the debate on how to construct an atomic bomb.[17]

Groves immediately recognized that he and Oppenheimer had complementary skills and drives. Oppenheimer had such a comprehensive grasp of the scientific issues in bomb construction that Groves knew he was absolutely

15 Rhodes, op. cit., pp. 443–47.
16 Rhodes, op. cit., pp. 119–27.
17 Rhodes, op. cit., pp. 443–47.

the best man to lead its design. He also had an 'overweening ambition,' which Groves believed could mesh with his own. It has been said that Groves, 'understood that Oppenheimer was frustrated and disappointed; that his contributions to theoretical physics had not brought him the recognition that he believed he deserved. This project could be his route to immortality.'[18] In addition, Groves understood that Oppenheimer would require more delicate handling than he was accustomed to lavishing on subordinates. Usually, Groves preferred to push and even taunt people to test their 'toughness;' if they did not 'measure up,' he simply pushed them out. With Oppenheimer, he deliberately set out to create a rapport akin to personal friendship.[19]

Groves believed in Oppenheimer so deeply that he was prepared to defend him even at the risk of his own career. For starters, Army counter-intelligence was concerned that Oppenheimer had a number of intimates who were identified as members of the Communist Party, including his brother and wife. Moreover, some argued that with so many Nobel laureates involved in the mission, perhaps the lab director should be one as well, which Oppenheimer was not. Would he, they worried, have sufficient authority? Only when Groves challenged these critics to find someone better did he win over the Army. In championing Oppenheimer, Groves even chose

18 Norris, Robert S. 'General Leslie R. Groves and the Scientists,' from the Preliminary Proceedings from the Atomic Heritage Foundation's Symposium on the Manhattan Project, April 27, 2002, p. 33.
19 Norris, Robert S. *Racing for the Bomb: General Leslie R. Groves, The Manhattan Project's Indispensable Man.* South Royalton Vermont: Steerforth Press, 2002, p. 237.

deliberately not to pass on all of the security information in his possession, including references to the fact that Oppenheimer's brother had been approached by a Soviet spy; a choice which naturally left Groves open to charges of treason. As a result of these choices, however, Groves established a deep and trusting relationship with his bomb design chief that was to last the rest of their lives.[20]

The starting place: attracting talent and building a team

Both Groves and Oppenheimer knew that recruiting the best talent was fundamental to success. Thanks to his intimate familiarity with the international physics community, Oppenheimer and his associates were able to identify the best people possible, by name, position by position. Aware of the curious mix of feverish ambition and high idealism amongst the scientists that he hoped to recruit, Oppenheimer created a powerful vision, arguing that their work promised to end the war and perhaps all future world wars as well; it was an opportunity, he claimed, to alter the course of history. His recruits bought into Oppenheimer's vision. As one participant put it:

> It was an unparalleled opportunity to bring to bear the basic knowledge and art of science for the benefit of [our] country . . . This sense of excitement, of devotion and of patriotism in the end prevailed.[21]

Groves, as well believed, 'first and foremost, [to] find and recruit the best people you can.'[22] What they had already

20 Rhodes, op. cit., pp. 448–49.
21 Rhodes, op. cit., p. 459, quote p. 452.
22 Norris, op. cit., pp. 192–193.

done was far less important than what they could do. In fact, in at least one instance, Groves cited lessons learned from Robert E. Lee in selecting talent:

> . . . select men much younger in years and with much less experience and reputation instead of deferring to normal practices. One of my two most important and successful selections was made against the strongest advice of all my most senior and valued advisors.[23]

Similarly, both remained involved, throughout the talent selection process and beyond. Oppenheimer remained extremely attentive to the needs and anxieties of project candidates. According to Feynman:

> He paid attention to everyone's problems . . . [h]e worried about my wife, who had TB, and whether there would be a hospital out there . . . he was a wonderful man.[24]

Groves' style, in turn, was always to ask: 'What can I do to make it easier for you to do your job?'[25]

Once the talent was identified and recruited, the remaining problem was how to build a team out of them. Given that America's nuclear physics resources were spread across the country – in politically powerful and competitive university departments in Berkeley, Chicago, and New York – it was only natural for many to argue that maintaining continuing parallel efforts in these dispersed settings was the most efficient way to go. Oppenheimer, on the other hand, argued that a central laboratory was a necessity because splitting up the talent would prohibit the intense

23 Norris, op. cit., pp. 137–138.
24 Feynman, Richard P. *Surely You're Joking, Mr. Feynman!* Bantam Books, 1985, p. 93.
25 Norris, op. cit., p. 203.

exchange of ideas and views that he sought. Groves agreed, adding that the project required strict isolation from the general populace for reasons of security. After a long search, they chose the campus of a defunct boys' school named 'Los Alamos' in New Mexico. Isolated it surely was, and many candidates for the project worried that the environment was inhospitable and lacked the sufficient cultural stimulation that they and their families desired. In addition, the scientists bristled at the security controls that the Army wanted to impose upon them.[26] Despite such concerns, the site decision was upheld and the security controls were enacted to the greatest degree possible.

The battle over compartmentalization vs. freely-flowing knowledge

Oppenheimer knew that for big scientific change to be achieved there would need to be both spontaneity and an open exchange of ideas, which had to be encouraged and yet controlled. The project had to be a place, 'where people could talk freely with each other, where the theoretical ideas and experimental findings could affect each other, where the waste and frustration and error of the many compartmentalized experimental studies could be eliminated . . . '[27] He believed that isolation by scientific discipline and narrow bureaucratic procedures could strangle idea flow, and would severely undermine a project with so many intricately-related issues. Every scientist and engineer, he hoped, would know what was happening, and as a result, be inspired to work towards a

26 Rhodes, op. cit., pp. 449–52.
27 Quotations from Rhodes, op. cit., pp. 449–51.

common goal, sometimes across disciplines. It was a delicate balance between openness and protection that many organizations find difficult to achieve.

While Groves was sympathetic to many of Oppenheimer's concerns regarding the need for free exchange of ideas and information – in fact, he and Oppenheimer spoke by phone every day – he nonetheless intervened with a heavy hand out of concern for military security and insisted that the policy of compartmentalization continue at Los Alamos. Because compartmentalization served Groves in the consolidation of his power – he was the only person with a systematic overview of the entire project from both scientific and administrative standpoints – this issue was a particularly difficult one for him to compromise on.[28]

Groves had already, in fact, identified certain individuals as security risks and wished to bar them from working at the Los Alamos site. Rather than obey compartmentalization, however, the scientists continued to discuss all problems freely, with whomever they chose. 'There was no way of telling beforehand,' Leo Szilard – one of the great physicists of the 20th century – later wrote, 'what man is likely to discover and invent a new method which will make the old methods obsolete.'[29] The process of invention, Szilard and others argued, required freedom of speech: the more scientists knew, the more likely it was that breakthroughs would be made, regardless of their designated area of compartmentalization.[30]

28 Norris, Robert S. *Racing for the Bomb: General Leslie R. Groves, The Manhattan Project's Indispensable Man.* South Royalton Vermont: Steerforth Press, 2002, p. 256.
29 As cited in Rhodes, op. cit., p. 503.
30 Rhodes, op. cit., p. 568.

Oppenheimer agreed with this philosophy of openness, and insisted that weekly progress reviews be open to everyone who was scientifically qualified. He also offered an alternative version of compartmentalization: the Army, he suggested, should take care of security and secrecy, while the civilian-run laboratory – the core of work at Los Alamos – would figure out how to design the bomb. Groves reluctantly agreed in principle, understanding that any further insistence on rigid compartmentalization would lead to unacceptable delays.[31] In a spirit of compromise, Groves allowed the scientists an unusual amount of freedom, while maintaining compartmentalization in the non-research related portions of the Manhattan Project.[32]

A pressure cooker that stretched individual performance

As several thousand scientists and engineers arrived in March 1943, Oppenheimer quickly emerged as a master administrator. Participants gathered for a series of 'introductory lectures' on the issues to be resolved. Their average age was 25, though there were a number of older men, eight of whom were Nobel laureates (with 12 more to follow).[33] Having long been barred by lack of membership in the project, or by compartmentalization, from learning what their colleagues had accomplished,

31 Rhodes, op. cit., p. 454.
32 Kevles, op. cit., p. 330.
33 Norris, Robert S. *Racing for the Bomb: General Leslie R. Groves, The Manhattan Project's Indispensable Man.* South Royalton Vermont: Steerforth Press, 2002, p. 625.

the young scientists were suddenly brought up to speed on developments they could only have guessed about. The mood was upbeat, even euphoric.[34]

The stakes were high, the time short, the work more demanding than any of these scientists had ever faced before, and it was all unfolding in front of the most elite 'stars' of their profession. To say stress was symptomatic of working in the Manhattan Project would be a gross understatement. It had all the characteristics of a pressure cooker. Early on, Oppenhimer decided to let individuals find their own unique ways of coping with the stress. Many of the staff had similar personality attributes: brainy, competitive, and somewhat socially inept. They were isolated in a remote location and communication with the outside world was limited by security constraints. They lived virtually on top of each other, and they simply couldn't avoid frequent contact. Few diversions other than social gatherings, horseback riding, and mountain hikes were available. Not surprisingly, such conditions inevitably led to imaginative ways of releasing tensions. Future Nobel laureate Richard Feynman taught himself to play a set of children's drums, which he had found abandoned, and which became a personal signature of his throughout the rest of his career. Along with others, Feynman also relied on pranks as a way of easing tensions. He was notorious for picking the locks of top-secret safes, where he left 'guess who?' notes; in fact, he was infamous for sneaking away from a meeting on security to break into the desk of Edward Teller, at the very moment that Teller was arguing how safe his papers

34 Rhodes, op. cit., p. 460.

were there.[35] But even in play, work was never far away. Some of the most important breakthroughs were made on hikes in the mountains, when staff members felt free to cross over into the 'compartments' of their colleagues.[36]

Organizing individual genius, wild ideas, and intricate work

Oppenheimer carefully choreographed the scope and pace of the intricately interrelated work. Calculations from the theoretical division determined specifications that the chemistry and armaments experts had to meet, which in turn set the parameters for the prototypes that the metallurgists had to machine. To create an effective administrative structure for these issues, Oppenheimer established teams based on the expertise of the scientists and engineers, which were then distributed into program categories, such as theoretical physics, experimental physics, chemistry and metallurgy, and ordnance.

Each category had a division leader, who broke the tasks down for smaller groups with their own respective leaders. It was a hierarchical arrangement, with division leaders reporting to the lab director, Oppenheimer; they met with him separately as well as together in the governing board, which was designed to provide an overview of all activities with a view to coordination.[37]

---

35 Feynman, op cit., pp. 69–71.
36 Rhodes, op. cit., p. 568.
37 Swanstrom, Edward. *The Manhattan Project: Knowledge Management Case Study*. eKnowledgeCenter.com, **www.metainnovation.com/researchcenter/courses/ Revised%20Manhattan%20Case/**

Regarding leadership for these divisions, Oppenheimer took care to choose the appropriate person rather than someone merely with seniority or the right title in civilian life. Starting with the all-star cast that had been assembled for Los Alamos, he tended to favor 'leaders' who had both social skills and the confidence to allow for the free-flowing interplay of ideas, and who were also systematic in their approach to problem solving. In this scheme, assuring the generation of good ideas was the goal, and personal feelings were irrelevant. For example, Hans Bethe was chosen over Edward Teller to head the theoretical program division, even though Teller had been occupied with the concept of an atomic bomb far longer than Bethe had and so enjoyed – and vociferously felt entitled to – seniority in the project. Oppenheimer's motivation in choosing him, Bethe believed, was that, '[my] more plodding but steadier approach to life and science would serve the project better at that stage of its development, where decisions had to be adhered to and detailed calculations had to be carried through, and where, therefore, a good deal of administrative work was inevitable.'[38] This decision deeply embittered Teller, who was regarded as highly creative, yet overly sensitive to what he perceived as slights.[39]

While the structure had to be flexible enough to tap into the wild ideas that were emerging unpredictably, Oppenheimer imposed strict deadlines on discrete projects to push the teams to move forward. With the basic design of the bomb undecided and under constant

38 As cited in Rhodes, op. cit., p. 539.
39 Ibid.

reformulation, the early period involved open-ended experiment and brainstorming. Scientists and engineers explored all options simultaneously and comprehensively, often in ways that disregarded the formal hierarchy. For example, taking advantage of the irrepressible Richard Feynman, who wasn't afraid to challenge the ideas of the 'great men' under whom he served, both Neils Bohr and Hans Bethe enjoyed bouncing ideas off of him before presenting them to the 'big shots.'[40] Oppenheimer also offered a weekly colloquium that was open to all. In this forum, he informed everyone present of the progress thus far and the issues that remained to be resolved. All participants were invited to share their own perspectives.

In an effort to keep alternative ideas flowing and perspectives fresh, Oppenheimer forbade the originators of ideas from claiming 'ownership.' Everyone was forced to work on the ideas of others. Revealing his frustration with this policy, Teller wrote: 'Almost constant collaboration was necessary, all the work done at feverish pace, and one's new idea, once hatched, could be taken away and given to others to develop . . . [It was] a little like giving one's child to someone else to raise.'[41]

Oppenheimer worked hard to keep the talent on board rather than allowing them to quit, in particular by relying on their sense of personal mission. In spite of his own significant individual gifts, Oppenheimer strove to eschew his own ego in making decisions and deploying resources.

40 Feynman, op cit., pp. 60, 87–88.
41 As cited in Herken, Gregg. *Brotherhood of the Bomb*. New York: Henry Holt, 2002, p. 85.

Despite his own conflicts with Teller, he still asked him to conceive and design the far more powerful fusion bomb (the 'Super') as the head of a subgroup within the theoretical division. The two of them also met once a week for discussions on Teller's ideas, which touched on a number of areas crucial to the current project's completion.

Oppenheimer created similar opportunities for others.[42] In a very real sense, Oppenheimer was relentless in his search for the best ideas for the project, and accordingly treated his scientists as knowledge professionals, consciously drawing them in and continually engaging their ideal for a higher purpose.[43]

The implosion alternative: how to keep a 'ridiculous' idea alive

Despite the apparent formality of the Manhattan Project, both Groves and Oppenheimer kept many 'wild ideas' alive alongside, or often in competition with, the main lines of research, a practice that in the end proved decisive to the success of the program. Groves believed that: '… if there was a choice between two methods, then build them both.'[44] This willingness to prototype ideas ensured that alternatives remained under development and available throughout the life of the program, rather than being easily dismissed as unsuitable or unworkable. In the area of detonation, it was long recognized that if the timing was off by a millionth of a second, the bomb might 'fizzle,'

42 Rhodes, op. cit., p. 546.
43 See **www.metainnovation.com/researchcenter/courses/Revised%20Manhattan%20Case/ManhattanCase.htm**.
44 Norris, op. cit., p. 232.

exploding with the force of 60 tons of TNT rather than the estimated 20,000. At the beginning of the project, the principal working model was a 17-foot 'plutonium gun' designed to shoot fissionable matter into the bomb base to create a 'critical mass.' Seth Neddermeyer suggested a different way: why not create a sphere that would implode evenly, squeezing the materials together from three dimensions? He argued that it would be faster and more compact, both practical battlefield considerations.[45]

Articulated at an open meeting, Neddermeyer's idea faced withering opposition from virtually everyone, including Oppenheimer. Not only would the implosion have to be perfectly symmetrical, many objected, but the core material might also squirt out instead of compress. Many younger scientists openly ridiculed the idea: 'It stinks,' Richard Feynman had said.[46] Others, who were entrenched proponents of the gun model, argued that their choice was the alternative most likely to succeed. However, in spite of his own doubts, Oppenheimer pulled Neddermeyer aside for a private conference and told him to look into the idea more thoroughly. He appointed Neddermeyer, who, like Teller, disliked cooperative efforts, to lead implosion experimentation and flesh out the extremely complex mathematical calculations that the generation of an 'implosion wave' would require. For more than a year, Neddermeyer did this in isolation, without rigid deadlines and shunning the give and take that most of his colleagues had come to accept as part of the working style of the project.[47] The result of this

45 Rhodes, op. cit., p. 466.
46 As cited in Rhodes, op. cit., p. 479.
47 Rhodes, op. cit., p. 467.

decision to support Neddermeyer's idea on a 'bootleg' basis was to prove greatly fortuitous for the project.

As the project moved into its second year, it became apparent that the gun model was unlikely to succeed. The implosion model, kept alive by Oppenheimer under the stewardship of Neddermeyer, emerged as perhaps the only feasible alternative available, though the technical challenges still appeared insurmountable. Morale collapsed and Oppenheimer considered resigning.[48] Solving the problem would require moving from issues of ordnance engineering to that of basic science: determining, in excruciating detail, the fluid dynamics of what would occur for a very few milliseconds at the moment of triggering the bomb. The implosion model was the only possible solution available to the team, but this, in turn, would require new perspectives on the problem; Neddermeyer was asked by Oppenheimer to give up his leadership role on what was originally his idea, and pass this project onto others for completion. Oppenheimer made this request of Neddermeyer, '... on behalf of the success of the whole project...'[49]

Leadership characteristics: superior intellect, human warmth

Both Oppenheimer and Groves placed themselves at the heart of everything, intimately involved – yet delegating tasks to the most qualified. They monitored *all* technical developments, and nothing of importance seemed to

48 Rhodes, op. cit., pp. 541–49.
49 Rhodes, op. cit., p. 547.

escape them. Both were adept at keeping their staff hard at work, listening to their problems sympathetically and offering suggestions while pushing them to stick to the deadlines. Both were constantly on them to exchange information. In addition, both engendered strong personal loyalty from the team, as if any failure on their part would be a disappointment to them.[50] It added up to a very effective leadership style. As Bethe recalled:

> [Oppenheimer] knew and understood everything that went on in the laboratory, whether it was chemistry or theoretical physics or machine shop . . . and fitted it into the general scheme of things and drew the right conclusions. There was just no one else in that laboratory that came even close to him . . . There was a human warmth as well. Everybody certainly had the impression that Oppenheimer cared what each particular person was doing. In talking to someone he made it clear that that person's work was important for the success of the whole project. I don't remember any occasion at Los Alamos in which he was nasty to any person, whereas before and after the war he was often that way.[51]

Similarly, John Lansdale, Groves' chief aide for security and intelligence matters, observed: '[Groves] … had a sort of catalytic effect on people. Most of us working with him performed better than our intrinsic abilities indicated.'[52]

Furthermore, the dual leadership role with Groves allowed Oppenheimer to claim the role of 'good cop' to Groves' 'bad cop,' and, as a result, much of the criticism that might have landed on him was deflected onto the General. By design, Groves was blamed for everything that went wrong.

50 Kevles, op. cit., pp. 330–31.
51 As cited in Rhodes, op. cit., p. 570.
52 John Lansdale as quoted in Norris, op. cit., pp. 235–236.

Conclusion

By January 1945, the Manhattan Project had cost $2.2 billion. Half-jokingly, General Groves warned the staff that if it did not work, 'each of you can look forward to a lifetime of testifying before Congressional Committees.'[53] In the desert a few months later, the bomb was successfully detonated, sending a fireball into the air with the force of 18,600 tons of TNT. The world had entered a new age, one of unusual promise and terrifying fears. Atomic bombs were built and used by the Allies to bring the war to a conclusion. Against all odds, a virtuoso team of all-stars was able to meet the challenge that their country had handed them.

Implications for leading virtuoso teams: Summary and Key Questions

Can you imagine what the world would be like today if Oppenheimer and Groves had failed to get the best talent from every possible source? Yet, in the corporate world, we are consistently surprised that when managers face big issues, they fail to get the most talented people to tackle those issues head on. In most cases that we see, from the very moment of project inception, compromises begin to be made about who can be on the team and why significant all-stars are unavailable. The Manhattan Project is a vivid reminder: if you want to achieve *big change*, recruit a virtuoso team.

Vision is a tricky thing, and very important when dealing with talented people whose intellectual energy is fueled by their emotions and personal aims. Oppenheimer realized that the vision he used to recruit great talent truly needed to resonate with each virtuoso performer. Oppenheimer also realized that without their complete

---

53 As cited in Kevles, op. cit., p. 332

buy-in to the vision underlying this high risk and exhaustive project, he'd fail as a leader to recruit or keep such talent together. While it can probably be argued that 'saving the free world' is an uncommonly compelling vision, and one that is typically more powerful than what most of us have to work with in everyday life, we are still struck by the fact that the visions we see within many corporate projects teams are those provided to them by 'the company,' or by someone from outside the team. These visions are often formulated without consideration of what they really – and we mean *really* – mean to the team members. Instead, we believe that one of the lessons of the Manhattan Project is that what is really needed is a vision to touch each virtuoso performer in a profound way.

Putting the great physicists together in one location – literally on top of each other day and night – was an important ingredient that helped harness their collective intellectual capital. Knowing great conversations can't happen without elbow-to-elbow contact, Los Alamos was born. We believe that virtuoso teams must frequently be co-located for as long as the project takes, if you are to get full value from the talent that you've assembled. Meeting for a few hours a day, or virtually, and then retreating back to separate offices won't work if you want to team up great talent to achieve *big change*. We believe that co-locating the team over extended periods into intimate physical space – to intensify idea flow through conversations and dialog – is one of the most important yet most avoided (because of the inconvenience it typically entails) tactics to drive talented teams to higher performance.

Oppenheimer realized the talent at his command was extraordinary, but unless he came up with organizing mechanisms to encourage individual thinking, spur appropriate idea flow, and ignite the occasional wild idea, then the project was doomed to failure. Attending to these details through the basic building blocks of organization – hierarchy, role clarity, reporting relationships, communication channels – was essential to get results beyond the individual talent potential and to reach the extraordinary results that were demanded.

Too often, high-powered teams are put together without thinking through the details of how they will work together and what the basic organizing principles will be. Alternatively, some managers are intimidated by great talent and shy-away from organizing it to its full effect. We believe that the story of the Manhattan Project and how it worked is a testimony to the power of 'the devil being in the details' – for any project – and shows that each detail must be attended to appropriately.

The endless struggle between idea flow and organizational complexity is also a leitmotif that runs through the Manhattan Project story. Clearly the need for more ideas was in direct contradiction to the need for project secrecy. In addition, there was the question of how to generate novel ideas when so many true and opinionated experts were part of the team. Neddermeyer's alternative implosion idea, for example, was ridiculed when he first proposed it, so why then did Oppenheimer keep it alive? Perhaps he respected Neddermeyer's genius – his raw talent – sufficiently to know he might be on to something? Perhaps he realized that a great team is about a divergence of ideas, not a convergence of thinking and ideas? Whatever the reason, the lesson for leaders of virtuoso teams is clear. There are times when even the wildest of ideas should be nurtured and cultivated, for their future value might be immeasurable. The virtuoso team leader has to make this call, sometimes betting on the unlikely in order to move more ideas, rather than fewer, forward. Personal pride is not the issue. Ideas are the currency for virtuoso teams, and wild ideas can lead to the biggest payoff.

As you address your own company's Manhattan Project destined to change your competitive landscape, consider the following questions:

1 If you are facing an urgent and vital challenge, are you recruiting the very best and most talented people?

2 Is the vision created for your virtuoso team a vision that is compelling to each and every single member personally and professionally?

3 Is your virtuoso team located in the right place and space to encourage the intense and emotional interaction and conversations required?

4 Are the conversations, dialog, and debate on your team happening with sufficient intensity and regularity to create the idea flow needed to catalyze innovation and creativity, and make your virtuoso team's vision a reality? Or, are bureaucratic roadblocks and other barriers stifling the movement of ideas?

5 Do you let wild ideas live on in the hope that they might be essential elements in the solution the virtuoso team is looking for?

4 Drive change inside and outside the team

Creating revolution on demand in Thomas Edison's invention factory

> [T]ime, hard work, and some good luck are necessary . . .
> It has been just so in all my inventions. The first step is
> an intuition and comes in a burst. Then difficulties arise .
> . . 'Bugs' . . . show themselves. Months of intense
> watching, study and labor are required before
> commercial success – or failure – is certainly reached.[1]
>
> Thomas Edison

A major invention every six months, a patentable innovation every ten days! Impossible? Amazing? Not at all! In fact, Thomas Edison set this timetable for his team and then fulfilled the challenge, and in doing so they changed the world at least three times (electric light, recorded and replayable sound, and sound on cinemagraphic film). What made Edison so successful was that he appreciated and employed the skills necessary to effectively create, lead, and manage virtuoso teams around a clear vision and robust processes. The virtuosos he brought together knew exactly what they were doing, what others had done, how to do it, and why (in stark commercial terms), and on the basis of such

1 As cited in Israel, Paul. *Edison: A Life of Invention*. John Wiley & Sons, Inc., 1998, p. 177.

information and talent they were able to change the world again and again. Central to Edison's secrets of success was the creation of an 'invention factory,' where prototyping, a culture of innovation, great people, leadership, and brand building were fundamental to the team's extraordinary achievement.

In this chapter, we'll see Edison and his virtuoso team in action in a fast-cadence environment: moving ideas around at amazing speed, taking risks, failing, learning, succeeding, and then doing it all over again. We'll also see a team where time and (physical) space were managerially manipulated in order to facilitate idea flow, and we'll see the benefits of being one of the world's great *risk-makers*. Despite the vintage of this experience, we believe that the lessons are as valid today as they were a century ago. How to drive these lessons into your own team and organization might be your first step towards creating your own virtuoso teams.

The myth of the lone genius

The light bulb has come to represent the 'eureka moment' of discovery or insight – the switching on of a light bulb above the head of a creative individual. Ironically, however, the invention of the incandescent light bulb actually involved scores of engineers and machinists working as a powerful team – testing thousands of materials, tweaking the design details in innumerable prototypes, and even creating the supporting technology for the commercially successful generation of electricity – under the leadership of a great research manager and visionary: Thomas Edison. It was not, as many believe, the product of one man's genius for 'tinkering,' but instead a pioneering corporate undertaking, which created the

exemplar of the modern industrial research lab, a
perfectly designed and equipped invention factory, as
Edison himself called it. Following the success of the light
bulb and electric-power infrastructure that he created,
Edison went on to establish a second invention factory
staffed with assistants of the highest caliber and equipped
with the most modern and comprehensive selection of
tools available, which was far larger than the original
facility. There, Edison and his team essentially invented
the modern entertainment industry (with phonographs
and 'talking' motion pictures), as well as creating the
foundation for a wide variety of industrial products and
processes that continue to underlie a substantial number
of contemporary technologies.

The early years: from newspaper boy to serial inventor

Thomas Edison was born in Ohio on February 11, 1847,
the youngest of seven children. His father worked at a
number of different enterprises to feed his family,
including farming and shingle making. A sickly child,
Edison was educated largely at home by his mother:
though he briefly attended school in 1859–60, he learned
to further his growing interest in science and mechanics
through books and, more importantly, through
experiments in a chemistry laboratory that he set up at
home. As Edison noted, books could, 'show the theory of
things [but] doing the thing itself is what counts.'[2] Edison
first went to work at the age of 12, first as a newspaper

boy on the local railway then, at 14 he began a career as a telegraph operator. It was only a decade later that he was a full-time inventor with the best-equipped experimental lab in the world.

Edison's initial years as an entrepreneur

It was on the train that Edison began to exhibit the character and skills of an entrepreneur. After only 6 months on the job, he had hired two boys to run news-stands that sold periodicals and vegetables, sharing the profits with them. To occupy the long hours of idle transit, Edison also set up a chemistry lab in one of the cars, which was short-lived after a spilled bottle of phosphorus caught fire and ended his experiments. His most successful early entrepreneurial initiative, however, employed the then high technology of the time: the telegraph. Having observed the intense interest of passengers in the daily events of the American Civil War, Edison sensed an opportunity during the battle at Shiloh in April, 1862. 'I then conceived the idea of telegraphing the news ahead,' he later wrote. 'I decided that instead of the usual 100 papers I could sell 1000.'[3] Although he lacked the funds to purchase that many papers wholesale, he persuaded the editor to give them to him on credit and, because passengers bid up the prices of his newspapers, he went on to make a whopping profit. Not only did this episode teach Edison the importance of marketing his ideas to the right executive, but it also instructed him in the power of the press.

2 Ibid., p. 12.
3 Ibid., p. 16.

'Tramp' telegrapher gaining valuable knowledge

After the success of his newspaper sales venture, Edison decided in 1863 to become an itinerant telegraph operator, traveling from city to city in search of work, a career he would follow for the next five years.[4] This role of the 'tramp' or 'traveler' was an important hallmark of idea sharing and diffusion, and provides a foretaste of Edison's commitment to any and all processes that helped him and his team receive more and better ideas, and move them quickly:

> The tramp lifted the young mechanic out of 'mental ruts formed by a long apprenticeship and a narrow circle of acquaintances'.[5]

Though he was largely self-taught, Edison had learned the rudiments of the telegraphy trade from a grateful operator, James MacKenzie, whose son he had rescued from an oncoming train. With his new skills, Edison joined what has been called: 'an elite fraternity of technical workers.'[6] Part of the culture of this fraternity was the study of electricity and the practice of experimentation to improve the operation of the technologies that these workers depended upon. Edison took this seriously and worked on night shifts so that he could spend his days studying in libraries and experimenting in his well-stocked amateur laboratory. Besides his technical studies, Edison, always hungry for knowledge, also studied Latin and Spanish.

4 Ibid., pp. 16–20.
5 Johnson, Elridge Reeves. 'The History of the Victor Talking Machine Company,' Feb. 1913, as quoted in Andre Millard, *Edison and the Business of Innovation*. Baltimore: Johns Hopkins University Press, 1990, p. 31.
6 Ibid., p. 21.

Soon he was sketching out a number of innovative ideas, such as a device to record incoming telegraph signals for slower delayed playback, which effectively eased the burden on harried operators like himself, while also ensuring greater accuracy of data transmission. Edison also invented techniques to send more than one message at a time over a single wire.[7]

According to Francis Jehl, one of Edison's early lab assistants: '[he] knew the secrets of electro-magnetism as no other man; he observed and studied while he tapped the keys; and the mysterious force so baffling to others was well understood by him . . .'[8] In other words, through practice, experimentation, and some book learning, Edison had achieved a unique, even intuitive, grasp of a revolutionary technology still in its infancy.

The inventor turns skilled networker to reach the market

Having set up shop in Boston as a telegrapher for Western Union, Edison began to work on his first true invention: an electric vote recorder. Already an expert at whipping up enthusiasm, he quickly garnered financial support from local capitalists. On June 1, 1869, Edison received his first patent for this invention. Unfortunately, his chosen market – local politicians – showed little interest in increasing the efficiency of role-call voting. In fact, because they needed time for vote-trading and lobbying, legislators preferred the traditional, slower system.

7 Ibid., pp. 22–28.
8 Jehl, Francis. *Menlo Park Reminiscences.* Kessinger Publishing Company, 1937, p. 234.

Undaunted by this failure and determined to better gauge his markets, Edison began to experiment on a variety of other projects, some of which took him further into the field of electric recording technology. Out of his renewed efforts, a rapid succession of products emerged, including a printing telegraph, double transmitters (the 'duplex'), and a fire-alarm telegraph. On the basis of this output, Edison resigned from his position at Western Union and posted a formal announcement in the *Telegrapher* that he intended to, 'devote his time to bringing out inventions.'[9] One key lesson, however, from the electric vote recorder, was a resolve to never again invent something for which there was no demand and no customers.

After the first blush of technical success, and despite receiving several additional patents and acquiring a growing appreciation of the complexity of the business environment, Edison once again failed to sell his ideas to customers. He then decided to move closer to his potential market, and moved to Manhattan, where the headquarters of the largest telegraph companies were located, and where there was a more innovative and product-hungry financial community than he had found in Boston. There, at the age of 22, Edison immediately began to work on establishing a network amongst the movers and shakers that he would need to befriend in the future. It was a new start that would prove decisive to his career.[10]

9 As cited in Israel, op. cit., p. 47.
10 Ibid., pp. 42–49.

The invention factory: replicating high performance teamwork

By 1869, while Edison's inventions were widely regarded as being the unpredictable output of an 'individual genius,' he was, in fact, hard at work in establishing a system to facilitate a team of talented individuals for producing a stream of successful inventions from his laboratory in Newark, New Jersey.[11] As a result of his frustration with the delays he incurred in his one-man laboratory in Boston, Edison had learned that in addition to a stably-funded work environment, he needed a machine shop that was constantly at his disposal to construct, test, and quickly redesign prototypes to develop his ideas. He also wanted to shorten conversational distances, by putting experimenters and machinists near enough to one another so that prototyping would become habitual.[12] One immediate benefit of such an arrangement was that as new and unforeseen problems arose, he could keep the machinists experimenting while he searched for alternative solutions.[13] A consummate prototyper, when confronted by a problem he could not solve, Edison simply switched to another project, perhaps to return to the original problem at a later time when new information or perspectives were available.[14] Ever optimistic, Edison viewed failure as a useful part of the process, offering lessons that could perhaps be applied elsewhere or that definitely proved a thing impossible. After over a

11 Ibid., p. 66.
12 Millard, Andre. *Edison and the Business of Innovation*. Baltimore: Johns Hopkins University Press, 1990, pp. 8 and 16.
13 Ibid., pp. 49–52.
14 Ibid., pp. 67–69.

thousand unsuccessful experiments and tests on one product, Edison once cheerily remarked to a disappointed assistant: 'We had learned for a certainty that the thing couldn't be done that way, and that we would have to try some other way.'[15] What this, of course, also meant was that Edison, as the leader or 'directing mind' of the process, had to find the right machinists and engineers to take part in it.

The culture that Edison sought to instill was that of the hands-on machine shop rather than a university lab concerned with advancing scientific theory. While respecting theory, Edison nonetheless refused to allow it to needlessly limit the range of his experiments; he accepted theories only after his own experiments or direct observations confirmed them.[16] Dogmatic theory, in this view, was dangerous in that it could function as a 'blinder,' hindering one from exploring solutions that contradicted it.[17] At Edison's lab, the focus was entirely practical and commercial. Summing up his method, Edison wrote:

> First . . . I find out if there is a need for the thing. Then I go and attack it in every way I can think out. This multiplied attack soon simmers down, until I get what might be called a composite idea – something which is a combination of all I have thought before, or else the one feasible idea which really seems to discount all the rest. Having once got started on what I think is the right track I keep up the pace until the goal is reached.[18]

15 As cited in McCormick, Blaine. *At work with Thomas Edison: 10 Business Lessons from America's Greatest Inventor.* Entrepreneur Press, 2001, p. 130.
16 Israel, op. cit., p. 95.
17 McCormick, op. cit., p. 79.
18 As cited in Ibid., pp. 96–97.

Despite his preference for practice over theory, Edison was also determined that his laboratories, or 'invention factories,' would act as a 'net to capture ideas from the many streams of technical innovation . . . '[19] Central to any such scheme was the library, which Edison placed in a prominent position in all of his plans for an efficient and effective innovation system.

Menlo Park and upgrading the team's capabilities

In 1874 Edison sold the rights to one of his inventions (the quadriplex telegraph, able to transmit four messages simultaneously on the same wire) for $30,000, using the funds to buy state-of-the-art lab equipment and to pay off a number of debts. Measured in monetary terms, this represented his greatest success to date. However, after a trip to England had demonstrated how little was known about the requirements for a safe and reliable electrical infrastructure, he concluded that a bigger and more complete laboratory was vital. It would have to have an excellent library to serve as a center for learned exchange, an open machine shop with the best available equipment, stocks of raw materials, and housing nearby for his many assistants.[20] The next year, he moved his Newark lab to the more secluded Menlo Park, 12 miles into the New Jersey countryside. In this secluded location, Edison famously predicted that he and his team would make, 'a minor invention every ten days and a big thing every six months

19 Millard, *Edison and the Business of Innovation*, op. cit., p. 9.
20 Israel, op. cit., p. 85.

or so.'[21] Though many of his contemporaries were thinking along the same lines, Edison's 'invention factory' was conceived on a far larger scale: with greater resources, he could work on more research tracks simultaneously – in 'countless variations' – and hence beat his rivals.[22] 'My one ambition is to be able to work without regard to expense,' he explained. 'What I want is a perfect workshop.'[23]

Selecting the team[24]

During the five years that the Menlo Park 'invention factory' functioned, over 200 men were at one time or another part of Edison's team. Originally, Edison was primarily interested in hiring staff to leverage his own intellect, but over time a real team of virtuosos emerged. At the inception of the Menlo Park facility, Edison already had a few favored experimental assistants that he had brought with him from Newark, including: Charles Batchelor, James Adams, William Carman, John Kruesi, Charles Stilwell, and Charles Worth, but he also knew that Menlo Park would need a much larger team for the projects he was beginning to envision. These men that Edison had brought with him were absolutely loyal to him – Batchelor had demonstrated a willingness to work up to 20 hours per day – and Edison shared royalties with several of them (Batchelor received 10% of all royalties

21 As cited in Ibid., p. 120.
22 Ibid.
23 As cited in Jonnes, Jill. *Empires of Light: Edison, Tesla, Westinghouse, and the Race to Electrify America*. Random House, 2003, p. 85.
24 This section relies upon Bernard S. Finn, 'Working at Menlo Park,' in William S. Pretzer (ed.), *Working at Inventing*, Baltimore: Johns Hopkins University Press, 2002.

and profits from his inventions, James Adams received 5% of royalties for the inventions that he was involved in, Francis Upton received 5% of the electric light royalties[25]). More importantly, Edison trusted in their problem-solving abilities and their motivation to persevere on their own, often with little direction; in a sense they formed a team within a team.[26]

With the qualities of these men in mind, Edison set about building a team by attracting great talent from around the globe. Many of them went on to become some of the great early industrialists of the electrical revolution.[27]

Edison was convinced that the set of skills he needed was taught less in schools than in apprenticeships on the shop floor. For him, real-world experience counted for far more than formal credentials.[28] In search of self-starters who could handle creative challenges on their own, Edison devised a number of ways to test them, including the assignment of menial jobs that required hours of solitary labor. For example, Francis Jehl had worked in the office of Edison's attorney and was fascinated by the great inventor. Jehl had pursued, in the night time hours, a rigorous study of chemistry and mathematics.[29] When his ambitions came to the attention of Edison, the young law clerk jumped, with the fervor of a child, at the opportunity to work in Menlo Park: 'It was like a wonderland to me,' he wrote, 'wherein the objects about

25 Israel, op. cit., p. 195.
26 This idea was first posed by Robert Freidel in a private conversation, May 2004.
27 McCormick, op. cit., pp. 82–83.
28 McCormick, op. cit., 82–83.
29 Jehl, op. cit., p. 16.

which I had been studying and dreaming had come to life.'[30] Edison immediately assigned him the task of cleaning and filling the cells of a primitive Bunsen battery, a dirty job that involved sulfuric acid, foul-smelling residues, and the intricate refitting of innumerable wire connections. After many hours, Edison himself inspected Jehl's work, commenting: 'Well, I see you know the ropes.' He was hired on the spot.[31]

Edison tested the thinking abilities of prospective employees, asking them questions they either couldn't answer or needed time to ponder. For ex-ample, he might ask: 'Where does the best cotton grow?' or 'What is the greatest depth ever reached in the ocean?' Rather than a correct answer, Edison wanted to observe how the candidate reasoned and how curious they were.[32] Furthermore, Edison might sabotage one of his prototypes, allowing prospective employees only a few minutes to find what was wrong; he then repeated the process *up to ten times* before hiring them.[33] If someone showed promise, he was offered the opportunity to start as a 'mucker,' that is, at the bottom of the lab hierarchy.[34] Edison preferred versatility in his employees rather than specialization, except in certain cases where highly technical or mathematical problem-solving was required. Machinists, for example, were expected to make anything upon demand – immediately and often without detailed explanations.[35] In spite of all of his tests, Edison literally

30 Jehl, op. cit., p. 33.
31 Jehl, op. cit., pp. 20–22.
32 As cited in McCormick, op. cit., p. 60.
33 Jehl, op. cit., p. 278.
34 McCormick, op. cit., p. 68.
35 Israel, op. cit., p. 274.

maintained an open door to talent; as long as they paid for their own materials, virtually anyone could enter the legendary lab to try his hand at inventing something. As a result, Menlo Park had a work culture that, 'stressed the skill of the worker and preserved the dignity and independence of his work.'[36] There was a tradition of 'inside contracting' within machine shops[37] that allowed fluidity in work – reminiscent of the 'marketplace for talent' idea that we've seen elsewhere in this book. This culture was so under-organized that Frederick Taylor, the father of 'scientific management,' was appalled to find that the workers actually ran many machine shops, and that Edison contracted with some of his own people on special projects.[38]

The work was tough, the hours were long; the typical workweek was six ten-hour days. The average stay at Menlo Park was three months, suggesting that such conditions were not for everyone; yet Francis Upton recruited Charles Clarke with the words: 'It is the chance of your life.'[39] There is no denying that Edison's fame became a magnet for talent, and bright young people from all over the world flocked to Menlo Park to work as part of Edison's team.

36 Millard, Andre. 'Machine Shop Culture and Menlo Park,' in William S. Pretzer (ed.), *Working at Inventing*, Baltimore: Johns Hopkins University Press, 2002.
37 Ibid., p. 52.
38 Ibid.
39 Finn, op. cit., p. 44.

The phonograph gives the team its first win

With the original team from his Newark lab, Edison's first major project for Menlo Park was the improvement of Alexander Graham Bell's telephone. Edison focused on enabling the telephone to operate over longer distances than Bell's original invention and significantly enhancing its audio quality as well. Then, combining the technology of the telephone and the telegraph, Edison and his team invented a prototype for a recording and playing phonograph – it worked on the first trial.

The following day, Edison and Batchelor took the crude prototype to the offices of the *Scientific American* magazine, astonishing the editors and eventually generating a thunderstorm of press coverage. This became a familiar pattern: announcing momentous success before the solution was even in view. Raising the stakes in public stretched his team, created an esprit de corps, sucked the venture capital away from competitors, and earned Edison the reputation of a heavyweight *risk-maker*. Ever willing to accommodate the press with folksy wisdom and long interviews with carefully selected reporters, Edison became known worldwide as 'the wizard of Menlo Park' and 'the Inventor of the Age.'[40] He went on to demonstrate the phonograph in person to US President Rutherford B. Hayes and his wife, later taking it to Europe and again astonishing the most famous scientists of the day in London and Paris. With these public-relations triumphs, Edison turned his attention next to the light bulb, as well as the entire infrastructure required for the use of

40 Israel, op. cit., pp. 142–47.

electricity on a city-wide scale. While the commercial development of the phonograph was shelved for some time in the far future, he continued to work on improvements to the telephone as well as other projects.[41]

Intuition guides the team

The arc light – a massive and intense incandescent light – was first constructed in 1809 in France. While able to light whole city blocks, most people were united in their belief that it was virtually impossible to adapt it for practical use in the home. The arc light was too big, too bright, too expensive, and perhaps it was even against the laws of physics to reduce its scale.[42] Nonetheless, after studying the problem for years, Edison had hatched a plan for home lighting: the high-resistance bulb. In spite of the skepticism of scientific experts, Edison began in 1878 to raise funds from corporate sponsors, including the young J.P. Morgan, for his experiments. Said one critic: 'It is a pity that Edison is wasting his time and energy and thought on incandescent lighting, which is sure to fail.'[43] In order to ultimately succeed, Edison would, it turned out, have to advance both basic scientific theory and

41 Ibid., pp. 148–155.
42 Jonnes, op. cit., p. 47. In technical terms, it was believed that the electricity powering the lights was impossible to subdivide into the smaller units required for less intense bulbs; additional problems included the lack of parallel circuitry – so if one light went out the whole string would, similar to Christmas lights – and the poor reliability and high operating expense of electricity generators. Edison's solution was based on Ohm's Law, a little-known hypothesis that was then poorly recognized in the established scientific community. The key for Edison was to create a high resistance lamp, which in turn would enable him to construct a parallel circuit.
43 As cited in Jehl, op. cit., p. 199.

engineering applications at the same time. Once again, he prematurely announced his 'success' to the press and then set about figuring out how to realize his idea. With his reputation on the line, he turned the resources of his entire lab to the challenge. Not only did they have to find the right materials for the bulb filament, they also had to create an entire system that would be able to compete with the prevailing gas lighting.[44] The search was exhilarating to this super-charged team.

The search for the right incandescent material

In spite of Edison's irrepressible optimism and the excitement of the chase, once the building of prototypes began, the task proved far more complex than had originally been imagined. A key problem was finding the material that was right for the filament; it had to have a long life and yet not cost too much. Starting with the chemicals and metals that Edison and his team knew from their telegraph and telephone experiments, they soon began to consider as many different prototypes as they could find, including many substances that scientific literature dismissed. Their procedure was to obtain samples and test them, often in the hope that under altered conditions they would behave differently than in previous tests.

Not only did Edison's agents gather tens of thousands of different raw materials worldwide to be tested as prototypes, from platinum to Japanese bamboo, but these

44 Ibid., pp. 233–34.

materials were also subjected to innumerable experiments, such as adding chemical coatings to alter their properties.[45] Jehl recounted these tests: 'The most interesting material of all . . . was the hair from the luxurious beards of some of the men of the laboratory. There was a great [betting] 'derby' . . . to see which would last the longer in a lamp.'[46] When they settled for a time on a platinum filament, its high cost drove Edison to scour the world for mines in order to increase supply, and reduce costs as a result. In this particular case, Edison had to contemplate new methods of ore refinement; but these efforts also failed.[47]

When the team discovered that a vacuum enormously increased filament life, Edison hired one of the world's most skilled glass blowers, Ludwig Boehm, whose stiffness made him the butt of many jokes. Despite this harassment, Boehm and the team developed perhaps the best vacuum technology then available in the world.[48] Eventually, Edison settled on carbon-coated filaments as the most economical, long-lasting, and energy efficient. After a brief demonstration of technical feasibility for his investors and a year-end display in 1880 for reporters and the public, Edison closed his laboratory doors to outsiders and began to concentrate on the commercial issues that his inventions left unaddressed.[49]

45 See Israel, op. cit., pp. 172–76.
46 Jehl, op. cit., p. 338.
47 Israel, op. cit., p. 184.
48 Jehl, op. cit., pp. 325–27.
49 Israel, op. cit., pp. 187–88.

Developing a commercial lighting system: building a team culture, a 'community of kindred spirits'

It wasn't enough to simply invent a viable incandescent light bulb, Edison had to also invent the entire systemic underpinnings for making money from such an invention: generators, distribution, fixtures, meters; an entire new system for delivering illumination was necessary. One consequence was that Edison had to now act as a research director, aware of everything that was going on, answering key questions, and checking on the progress of various interrelated projects. It was left to others to do the work of building and testing prototypes.[50]

At the beginning of 1880, Edison had over 60 employees of the very highest caliber. After having worked on the invention of the light bulb, they had grown into a unified team of uniquely motivated young men, with Edison – a ubiquitous presence – accepted as one of the boys and yet still the authoritative leader. The handful at the top of the lab hierarchy were known as the 'live-wire Edisonians' and got the most interesting work as well as a share of the profits. Lower-level employees were paid considerably less, as it was assumed that their enthusiasm and hopes for advancement formed the basis of their commitment. Edison's employees were always on call, and while expectations of them were at times impossibly demanding, the atmosphere of the lab was informal and freewheeling. It has been remarked that Edison's labs were noisy, crowded places that often seemed on the point of uproar.

50 Ibid., p. 191.

As he once told a new employee, the muckers did not work to any rules or regulations, because they were trying to achieve something.[51] As Charles L. Clarke related:

> Laboratory life with Edison was a strenuous but joyous life for all, physically, mentally and emotionally. We worked long night hours . . . frequently to the limits of human endurance . . . The psychological atmosphere of the place partook of the inspirational . . . a little community of kindred spirits . . . enthusiastic about their work, expectant of great results . . . often loudly explosive in word, emphatic in joke and vigorous in action . . . isolated as they were in the monotony of a rural neighborhood.[52]

Singing together was commonplace as was working all night long. Said Jehl: 'Our midnight lunch was a time of revelry; and when it was ordered, we knew that Edison was going to plow through the night without respite.'[53] However, if someone proved too difficult to work with, or went against the grain of the laboratory's culture, after a few warnings Edison might abruptly force him out. This is what happened to the glass blower, Ludwig Boehm, who had never fit into the Menlo Park culture.[54]

Creating a team process to drive high performance

According to Jehl, Edison planned the development of the commercial lighting system in a manner similar to that of Napoleon I for a military campaign. He envisioned all of

51 Millard, op. cit., p. 56.
52 As written for Jehl, op. cit., pp. 857–58.
53 Ibid., p. 285.
54 Israel, op. cit., p. 193.

the elements that had to come together before he began, and then took each step methodically. 'Like Napoleon,' Jehl wrote, 'he first planned his strategic campaign and then fought the battle; he never rushed forward without knowing what to do.'[55] In practical terms, unlike his other inventor-competitors, Edison had thought far beyond the lamp itself (and in particular the choice of filament material), to the entire system and infrastructure that the lamp would require, including the range of conditions (both industrial and domestic) under which it might be operated. He decided that he had to develop the following elements in concert:

1. an efficient generator of electricity;

2. an electric meter for 'registering the current;'

3. a mode of regulating the system;

4. an underground conducting system; and

5. peripheral equipment, such as sockets, switches, fuses, and wire insulation.[56]

As director of research, Edison divided the various tasks between his lab assistants and delegated items to teams of researchers and machinists. While Edison popped up unexpectedly to ask them questions, and kept detailed records of every aspect of the operations to gauge their progress, he typically left his teams largely on their own. They were free to come and go as long as the work was accomplished according to plan. In his words:

55 Jehl, op. cit., p. 244.
56 Ibid., pp. 232 and 243.

> I generally instructed them on the general idea of what I
> wanted carried out, and when I came across an assistant
> who was in any way ingenious, I sometimes refused to
> help him out in his experiments, telling him to see if he
> could not work it out himself, so as to encourage him.[57]

While, in fact, most of the 'key insights' originated with
Edison, he also listened to his team and was completely
open to their suggestions. The atmosphere in the laboratory
was one of total candor. In the maelstrom of ideas that
emerged during prototyping, it became increasingly
difficult to distinguish precisely where the ideas originated
or who had solved a given problem. Some of the live-wire
Edisonians, in particular Batchelor, were allowed to patent
details and specific applications of their contributions,
though Edison reserved the broader patent rights for
himself in order to minimize the complications that co-
authored patents posed for their holders in that era.[58]

The closing of Menlo Park

The elements of the Edison electric system were developed
in rapid succession and more or less according to plan. As
with the improved vacuum pumps, Edison's team
produced a dazzling array of technological innovations,
many of which were patented. According to Jehl, Edison,
'succeeded in developing a dynamo of revolutionary
design and unbelievable efficiency to generate current . . .
'[59] Edison also experimented with electric motors for
daytime use in such devices as elevators, sewing
machines, and even an electric railway.[60]

57 As cited in Israel, op. cit., p. 192.
58 Ibid., pp. 191–200.
59 Jehl, op. cit., p. 264.
60 Israel, op. cit., p. 198.

In the spring of 1881, when the basic experiments for his electrical system were completed, Edison turned his attention to the details of manufacturing them. While his Menlo Park lab remained open for some time – experimentation continued, but it was oriented towards solving mass manufacturing issues – Edison was moving his operations into Manhattan; this was a better location to attend to the business-oriented details of setting up a series of companies for the purposes of industrial production. At this stage, many of the elite, live-wire Edisonians were offered manufacturing partnerships in the technologies that they helped to pioneer. John H. Vail, for example, was hired in 1880 to tend to 11 dynamos simultaneously. Having accomplished his job, the following year he was put in charge of Edison's lighting plant in Manhattan and went on to become a lead advocate of the system in other parts of America.[61] Even Batchelor, Edison's most intimate and trusted collaborator, departed in order to run the company's operations in Paris. It was the end of an era.[62] After Menlo Park, Edison continued to be a vital force in worldwide technology, but he never again recaptured the invention factory 'magic' of the Menlo Park days.

Implications for leading virtuoso teams: Summary and Key Questions

Not only was Edison tireless in his intense interpersonal interaction with his team on a day-to-day basis, but he also understood the vital nature of building strong ties with key external sources of reputation,

61 Jehl, op. cit., pp. 547–48.
62 Israel, op. cit., pp. 199–202.

wealth, and know-how. Leaders of virtuoso teams must manage the outside as intensely as they manage the inside. Their own personal brands as perceived by external players are vital in acquiring talent and financial resources. Being able to manage and manipulate the press or other information sources is also essential.

Edison's team was not only great for what they actually *did* achieve, they may have been even greater for what *others thought* they achieved. Ensuring recognition for any virtuoso team may be key to ensuring a pipeline of great talent, ample money, and strong brand reputation, all of which are vital assets available to a virtuoso team that is trying to ignite *big change* in your organization.

Getting great talent may be the biggest challenge any virtuoso team faces. Creating a team image that acts as a powerful magnet for talent is essential for any long-term success. Edison's muckers, and most of the virtuoso teams in this book, all had leaders that recognized that only the very best talent is acceptable. That only the very best talent will make sure that their dreams of change become a reality. Far too many teams that have *big change* as part of their agenda simply do not have the talent necessary to achieve it, or if they do have the talent, it is constrained by organizational or leadership experiences which diminish it. We can spend forever defining what we mean by talent, but it clearly includes people brimming with the skills and energy needed to excel in their roles on the team. High energy, strong push, deep expertise, high self-confidence, and determination are also all hallmarks of great virtuoso team performances. Remember that Edison tested his team's talent relentlessly, making them show their desire, ambition, and skill, and he created an organization and work environment that made it easy for them to then do this. Although this may not be completely feasible in every situation, we believe that there is something to be borrowed here for any leader attempting *big change*.

Instilling a strong culture of pride, meritocracy, openness, and achievement are often the lifeblood of any virtuoso team. The time Edison spent with his team; those late evenings playing the piano and singing, or ordering in food for meals, or carefully planned practical jokes; the reference to 'muckers' as members of the team –

all contributed to a powerful culture. Edison's insistence that all team members be candid and that achievement be the basis for working on the most important projects helped build an open environment where direct conversation was the norm and individuals were valued based on their talent, not on their seniority or title. With virtuoso teams, taking time to create a strong culture is also required. Edison knew that talent, idea flow, and cooperation were essential. He built a culture to enable it. On your virtuoso teams, knowing the formula for success and building a culture to mirror and promote it are equally essential.

Edison also understood that high achievement took more than teamwork – it would take a team process. Prototyping stands out for us as a fundamental element of Edison's team and other teams we have examined. Whether they be physical prototypes, drawings, models, or role-playing to illustrate elements of the *big change* in mind – prototypes are essential as a valuable process tool for many virtuoso teams. Prototypes allow teams to come up with bold, provocative, and interesting ideas. Prototypes almost always fail one way or another, allowing for rapid learning and further refinement of ideas. Prototypes are a way to mitigate risk so that solutions and approaches underlying the change can be tested early to make sure they are not far off the mark. Prototyping is a valuable competence that many virtuoso teams deploy and it's not so much about the skill of prototyping, as it is about attitude. Prototyping recognizes that learning is best achieved by experimentation, rapid learning, trial and error, and that bold change can best be supported at times with bold prototypes along the way.

Edison's leadership and powerhouse team highlight a series of questions that any manager should answer when launching their own virtuoso teams:

1 Is the leadership of your virtuoso team focusing their energy inside and outside the team; inside to build the culture and drive the action; and outside to build the brand and personal network needed for success?

2 How does leadership of your virtuoso team spend their time? What does their diary look like? Is time – the most precious

resource – spent with the team and with key outside people? It is very easy to get time trapped and eaten up by the bureaucracies, which are very inward-looking. Leadership of a virtuoso team is not done on the 14th floor with the team working on the 4th.

3 Does your virtuoso team have the very best talent? And what are your leaders doing to make sure that the virtuoso team is a magnet for talent, and that the talent is tested to make sure it's exactly what the team needs?

4 Do your virtuoso teams prototype again and again? Test out their ideas in imaginative ways to elicit feedback and bring in new ideas and insights? Do they have an attitude that they'll figure it out (if so, Warning!) without outside help or do they use prototypes to propel the change forward?

5 Do you have a robust and total system for delivering big change that your virtuoso teams can employ to succeed? Does your system involve the careful use of space and time? Does it move ideas relentlessly so that they are tested, refined, and enhanced?

5

Going faster by knowing more

Roald Amundsen's team learns its way to polar success

If we are to win, not a trouser button must be missing.
Roald Amundsen

Cold, dark, and forbidding all describe the South Pole at the beginning of the 20th century. During 1910–12, two teams were in direct competition for the prize of being the first to reach what was possibly the last unexplored area in the world. The winning team, led by the brilliant Norwegian explorer Roald Amundsen, is a study in extraordinary leadership and managerial accomplishment. Against a much better-funded British team, led by the skilled Robert Falcon Scott, Amundsen assembled a virtuoso team.

In this chapter we'll learn key points important to many virtuoso teams. We'll see how Amundsen invented and adapted a wide array of different, imaginative technologies, created a powerful learning organization, inspired cooperation and collaboration amongst a team of very talented individual specialists, carefully selected each team member and utilized their skills to the utmost, conducted nearly flawless project planning, and displayed considerable communication skills. We'll see how Amundsen went about identifying and recruiting some of the world's best professionals from a variety of disciplines; how he forged these individuals into a lean and effective team whose competitive advantages included speed, intelligence and know-how, cooperation and leadership. The lessons illustrated here serve as powerful prescriptions for managers across the entire spectrum of organized activities, and offer timeless insights into what it means to take talent and deploy it effectively against a much stronger competitive adversary. This is truly a situation where the team was capable of achieving considerably more than the individuals themselves could envisage; a situation made much more interesting because Amundsen himself could clearly not lead by example in many of the disciplines involved.

This chapter will also illustrate important characteristics in many of the leaders of virtuoso teams that we have studied. Commitment to excellence, learning, and preparing for success were the hallmarks of Amundsen's professional life. His career had been spent preparing to reach the North Pole, from studying the survival techniques of Eskimos to devising nutritional strategies for preventing scurvy. Amundsen was totally obsessed with leading a team in groundbreaking polar exploration, and to accomplish this mission he always sought to learn from each of life's experiences. He was also a natural leader, running a ship without strife and inspiring his men to follow him into danger and the unknown. Amundsen's challenges are not strangers to today's leader, who may have to create teams of elite knowledge professionals and win against stronger competitors in highly uncertain and volatile markets. What can you learn from Amundsen's and his team's race to the South Pole? How did he lead? How did he manage this 'breakthrough project?' How did he apply lessons from the past to his own project? Amundsen's leadership of this virtuoso team and bold project are textbook illustrations of how to grapple with many management challenges you face today.

Becoming an Arctic learning professional: learning as a personal competence

At age 15, Roald Amundsen read Sir John Franklin's account of his Arctic expedition and immediately set out to learn all he could about polar exploration. 'Oddly enough,' he wrote, 'it was the sufferings that Sir John and his men had to go through which attracted me most . . . that got me to see myself as a kind of crusader in Arctic exploration.'[1] Already steeped in the national ski culture, Amundsen sought the advice of his Norwegian compatriots.

Amundsen was a disciple of Fridtjof Nansen, arguably the most famous Arctic explorer of the age. In place of the large-scale teams that were then popular, Nansen was pioneering a leaner, more mobile team kind of Arctic travel. This left a lasting impression on Amundsen, but he sought other mentors as well, including Eivund Astrup, who argued that 'primitive people' had much to teach their civilized contemporaries about survival techniques and practices.

Believing in the value of learning by experience, Amundsen sought out Arctic 'apprenticeships.' Early on, with Adrian de Gerlach onboard the *Belgica*, he took part in one of the first extended stays in Antarctica. By the winter of 1898 the ship had frozen into a massive ice drift off the coast of the continent. Shifting ice was threatening to crush it. Worse yet, in the 24-hour darkness, the crew was growing more and more depressed. Scurvy, the

---

1 As cited in Huntford, Roland. *Scott and Amundsen: The Last Place on Earth.* London: Abacus, 2002, p. 19.

deadly nutritional disease that few explorers understood at the time, had struck. Every member of the crew was suffering in a 'little private hell.'[2] Disaster, it seemed, was imminent, but Amundsen remained undaunted. For nine months he was marooned on the freezing ship, but he had learned a lot. He had kept largely to himself, and had taken copious notes about everything he saw. And he survived – with detailed notes that he could study to prepare for his own Arctic assaults.[3]

What had Amundsen learned? To begin with, he had studied the leadership of Captain Adrian de Gerlach. Amundsen despised de Gerlach as a weak martinet, and he reviled the poor cohesion of the crew. As a result of this intensely personal experience, Amundsen began to think about what it took to effectively manage a team in difficult circumstances. During his nine months of polar darkness, Amundsen also initiated a series of ongoing experiments to improve the equipment that was used. With his shipmate, Frederick Cook, he invented a new kind of 'aerodynamic' tent better suited to the windy local conditions. He also tested various clothing materials for arctic conditions. In his journal he coolly recorded the details of his swollen gums and the frightening mood swings associated with scurvy. On board the *Belgica*, Amundsen witnessed what he regarded as needless deaths. And he concluded that Arctic expeditions could avoid loss of life and unnecessary risks – with meticulous preparation. Taken together, he was learning systematically from the mistakes and oversights of past

2 Huntford, op. cit., p. 61.
3 Huntford, op. cit., p. 61.

explorers.[4] Even when he was involved in historic achievements, such as his participation in the first Antarctic sledge journey, Amundsen kept his journal focused on lessons he was learning: he refused to exult in his own glory, preferring instead to analyze in detail what he observed.[5]

First command and leadership: the Gjoa

After the *Belgica*, Amundsen sought ever more intense experiences on which to build his treasury of key knowledge. He went to Tromso (northern Norway) to learn from the 'Arctic skippers.' So single-minded was he that he shunned the company of all but the most experienced sealers and whalers. Some scoffed at his interest in these clannish, taciturn men, but Amundsen was unstoppable. 'There is nobody so stupid,' he noted, 'that he does not have something sensible to say.'[6] Amundsen wanted to get the most out of his Tromso opportunities, so he spent his entire inheritance on the *Gjoa*, a small sealing ship. He hired a seasoned crew and, in April 1901, took to the sea. To cover the cost of the trip, he and his crew hunted Arctic sea game. For five months, Amundsen lived like the Arctic skippers, eating seal steak and other catches. Financially, Amundsen 'only' broke even on this 'training' but technically, as the Commander, Amundsen learned many lessons about Arctic shipping from the local professionals. That they 'lived off the land,' he concluded, was crucial information. Further, commanding a small,

4 Huntford, op. cit., p. 68.
5 Huntford, op. cit., p. 57.
6 Huntford, op. cit., p. 72.

specialized crew bolstered his conviction that Nansen's 'new method' of Arctic exploration by drifting in the polar ice, followed by a mad sled dash to the pole and then back to the moving ship, was the model he should follow – for its efficiency and speed.

This streamlined approach stood in stark contrast to the conventional wisdom, in which huge teams were organized on a near-military scale with multiple redundancies and hence, many more mouths to feed.[7] Nansen's method meant, as one observer wrote: 'limiting the number of participants, and selecting a small party able to achieve the greatest possible degree of physical stamina: a small, trained group, in which all keep pace with each other in the coming trials.'[8]

Building a powerful team

Amundsen also continually worked to improve his leadership skills. In 1903, on an expedition to find a northwest passage, Amundsen had his first major command. And it was now that he discovered that he could, by natural inclination, run a 'happy ship,' where the team came together to harness the talent of all. He demanded absolute loyalty, sworn in an oath. But rather than relying on rank and hierarchy, he strove to *earn* his crewmembers' trust and respect. Amundsen developed a way of selecting and planning human resources that eliminated the need for bureaucracy and elaborate rules – his crew operated with a clear sense of both immediate

7 Huntford, op. cit., p. 29.
8 Ludvig Schmelck, as cited in Huntford, op. cit., p. 24

purpose and overarching mission. All team members knew what they were supposed to do. Amundsen trusted them to play their roles, so he rarely had to issue orders. The result was akin to a community functioning as a 'little republic.'[9]

Amundsen realized the right talent and personality mix would make or break an expedition's success. He chose his team – individual by individual – with extraordinary care. He tested them for their mix of skills *and* their initiative. Since he was seeking an indefinable 'fit' of character, he had to make intuitive snap judgments of personal suitability. In one example, Amundsen asked a potential recruit to pack fish into a crowded storage hull. When the man told him that it was impossible because of a lack of space, Amundsen summarily dismissed him. 'There's no space for you either on board this ship,' Amundsen is reported to have said.[10] He also refused to accept unqualified adventurers, misfits, 'hacks,' or anyone who might bring disaffection into the small group. He preferred a crew of the highest professional caliber and he paid top wages.

The Eskimos: learning from experts

During the winter of 1903, which Amundsen spent in Greenland while seeking to discover a northwest passage, he apprenticed himself to the local Eskimos. His interest and open-mindedness were extraordinary for that age of colonial imperialism, in that Eskimos were regarded as a primitive – hence 'inferior' – Stone-Age people in need of

9 Huntford, op. cit., p. 84.
10 As cited in Huntford, op. cit., p. 85.

civilizing influences. Instead of dismissing them as being uninteresting, or assuming the burden of improving them, Amundsen was determined to learn everything that he could from them, about their technology, habits and culture. After all, they lived in the polar regions, and thrived. Upon his first contact with the Eskimos, he set about earning their trust and mastering their language.

At each step of the way, Amundsen recorded observations for later study in his usual meticulous style. He studied the psychology of the Eskimos' dogs: rather than beasts of burden like horses, he came to believe that they were intelligent companions that required coaching and cultivation as intimate partners. He recognized that the Greenland variety of husky was superior to those of Siberia. He then decided to use only the former in his Arctic journeys. Amundsen also examined the natural garments of the Eskimos: unlike the synthetic fabrics available in the industrial world, he concluded, the Eskimos' fur coats and pants allowed air to circulate and hence prevented the heat-dissipating sweats that could become dangerous during the physical exertion of Arctic travel.

Amundsen became expert at constructing igloos, the hardy Eskimo shelters that rely entirely on materials immediately available in the Arctic tundra.[11] Finally, he carefully observed how Eskimos conserved their energy. Many European observers had concluded that they were sluggish and perhaps inherently lazy, but Amundsen realized that they were expertly pacing themselves, refusing to exceed a comfort zone that left them ample reserves of energy in

11 Huntford, op. cit., pp. 85–90.

case of emergency,[12] in a world where the next problem could well be around the next corner. In spite of these invaluable findings, Amundsen did not look to slavishly imitate the Eskimo. With an eye to boosting his efficiency and enhancing his margins of safety, he created his own synthesis, experimenting ceaselessly along the way to find the most appropriate mix of techniques. For example, Amundsen believed that skis, unknown to the Eskimo, are the best means of Arctic locomotion for men and allowed his team to keep up with dog sledges. At the same time, he concluded that the Eskimo diet of fresh meat represented the best hedge against the development of scurvy. This flatly contradicted the established medical opinion of the time. To augment fresh meat, Amundsen relied on pemmican (a cake of dried pounded meat mixed with fat) and chocolate as dietary staples, both of which he had specially prepared to avoid losing their nutritional value during processing.

Failure and success: all experiences contribute to leadership abilities

Amundsen learned from his successes, but also from his failures. After having wintered in Greenland, Amundsen set off in the spring of 1904 to find the magnetic North Pole. This was the scientific part of his journey. By some obscure miscalculation and in terrible traveling conditions, he missed his goal by about 30 miles; not a large amount by the standards of his era, but this failure weighed on him for the rest of his life.[13] Nonetheless he

12 Huntford, op. cit., p. 98.
13 Huntford, op. cit., p. 99.

valued the experience since, again, it was a fountain of new ideas and knowledge. At this point, Amundsen could now prepare and lead a traveling team in virtually any Arctic condition, from wet slush to the most frigid ice storms.[14] After a second winter in Greenland, Amundsen's team went on to be the first ever to discover a northwest passage. While this secured Amundsen a place in history, accomplishing something that such giants as Magellan and Columbus had been unable to do, he had his mind and heart elsewhere. Amundsen saw the northwest passage not as a major historical achievement, but as the completion of his 'Arctic apprenticeship'. This marked the end of the first step in his life's work. Up next was the conquest of the North Pole. He was in his early 30s.

Flexibility in creating stretch targets: Pole-reversal

Amundsen was stunned when he opened the newspaper on September 1, 1909. Headlines read that Cook, his good friend from the de Gerlach expedition to Antarctica, had 'discovered' the North Pole. To make matters worse another American, Robert Peary, soon put in a rival claim, announcing that he had beaten Cook to the North Pole. This generated a controversy that has lasted to this day. Nonetheless, the allure of the North Pole had been compromised.

The claims regarding the North Pole forced Amundsen's hand. His dream of being first was obliterated. He had to decide quickly how to respond, since he had firm plans to

14 Huntford, op. cit., p. 100.

make a scientific expedition to the North Polar basin (and Pole itself) in 1910. It didn't take long for Amundsen to shift his entire focus. He decided immediately – and in secret – that he would go to the South Pole instead. No one was to know. His new objective was only to be announced *after* departure. The surprises weren't over. Two weeks following Amundsen's secret decision, the British Naval Captain Robert Falcon Scott formally announced his intention to journey on his famous ship, *Terra Nova*, to the South Pole in 1910. To gain a tactical advantage over Scott, Amundsen's secret had to remain closely guarded. Neither his powerful mentor, Nansen, nor his financial supporters, nor anyone in the Norwegian government, knew that Amundsen was now heading due south. A race was on, in complete stealth.[15]

Preparation and plan

Not surprisingly, Amundsen's first step was to learn what he could from others who had been in the Antarctic region. Amundsen completed a dispassionate, in-depth analysis of the recent experience of Ernest Shackleton in Antarctica. Although Shackleton was heralded as a daring hero, Amundsen focused on the expedition and not the man. He viewed it as a near disaster. He concluded the expedition had made a number of significant mistakes. The supply depots were too few, too small and inadequately marked. This greatly reduced safety margins. A missed depot would have immediately become a matter of survival. Man-hauling slowed and exhausted Shackleton's team, which

15 Huntford, op. cit., pp. 205–8.

was perhaps the principle reason that he failed to reach the South Pole. Finally, though dogs were taken, no one knew how to handle them properly and hence they were a costly waste. From these lessons, Amundsen concluded that his own combination of a small, elite team using skis and dog-pulled sledges was the right one. He believed that heroism and courting danger while seeking adventure reflected poor planning. His team would advance slowly at a carefully chosen pace. No stone would be left unturned in the planning process. Reasonable goals would allow plenty of physical and mental rest.

Though careful planning was the norm, bold strokes providing real advantage were not ignored. On the basis of careful study of previous expeditions and available data, Amundsen chose to land on the uncharted Ross Ice Shelf. If the shelf proved to be fast-moving ice, the expedition would fail. If it proved stable, on the other hand, the gain would be significant. He took the calculated risk. It shaved 120 miles or 9% off the round trip from the expedition. Scott's decision was to follow a more established route.[16] The devil is in the details. Amundsen left none unaccounted for. With his secret plan laid out, Amundsen personally oversaw every aspect of implementation. He supervised the purchase, and often the manufacture, of the equipment and provisions. Extraordinary attention was paid to key items that addressed particularly risky aspects of the project. For example, food would be homemade, specially packed, and would combine pemmican with Arctic meats that they would hunt. No commercial food

16 Huntford, op. cit., pp. 242–45.

would do, given the need to maintain strength, alertness, and health under the harshest conditions.

For his team, Amundsen wanted 10 or fewer men. Each would be a skilled specialist. Each would play a clearly-defined role on the team. They were psychologically as well as physically fit. They had a proven ability to adapt and learn quickly. Amundsen knew the value of great talent and was willing to pay for the best. He hired an expert dog driver and two highly-experienced ice sailors, thereby building in redundancy for critical skills. He even discovered a cook who could prepare seal meat in a variety of tasty ways, in anticipation of the months of isolation ahead. In particular, judging him a splendid as well as useful companion, Amundsen engaged the champion skier Olav Bjaaland, who was also an expert carpenter and, for leisure, a violin maker as well.

Bjaaland's selection to the team was not only based on filling a skill need, it was also a carefully considered symbolic move. Realizing that he was asking the entire team to achieve a true stretch goal, Amundsen felt that his own personal skills in skiing, an essential competence, were not top-notch. To remedy this potential leadership weakness, Amundsen found Bjaaland. By recruiting the very best individual at skiing based on his tremendous expertise as opposed to title or hierarchy, worthy of following and held in the utmost esteem by fellow Norwegians, Amundsen was in effect saying that: 'if you (the collective team) doubt my leadership skill, then certainly you will follow Bjaaland on our journey to the Pole!'[17]

17 Private conversation with Roland Huntford, September 2004, Lausanne, Switzerland.

The sole exception to his rule of personal selection was Hjalmar Johansen, a veteran of Nansen's Arctic expeditions. Because Johansen judged himself the stronger skier and more experienced explorer relative to Amundsen, there was friction between the two from the start. Amundsen felt compelled to invite Johansen to join his team because of a commitment to Nansen made in return for the use of the ice-boat *Fram*. To be fair, Amundsen tried hard to win Johansen over. He realized that Johansen had saved Nansen's life and he felt an obligation to his patron.[18]

All or nothing: stretch, stretch and more stretch

Upon embarking from Norway, Amundsen's team knew nothing of the plans to head to the South Pole. They still thought that they were ultimately heading north – to the North Pole. Amundsen wondered if the team would remain with him when they discovered the truth. Correctly reasoning that he would be recalled if his patrons learned of his new destination, he carefully timed the revelation of his secret change of plans until they had reached a point of 'no recall.' In spite of the quality and trustworthiness of his team, he had informed only his brother and the officers of the *Fram* of his plan to conquer the South Pole rather than the North Pole.

The team set sail south without fanfare in April 1910. At that time, to make the North Pole required initially heading south around the Cape of Good Hope (South

18 Huntford, op. cit., pp. 248–51.

America) and then back to Alaska, where a drift with the polar ice across the Arctic region would commence. That they were initially sailing south for some time would be of no concern to the team; they expected it as the way that they would make their way north. But, off the coast of Portugal, Amundsen decided that the time had come to reveal the plan to the men. Standing on the deck of the *Fram*, with a map of the Antarctic region fixed to the mast, he informed the crew of his new plans, and the reasons for them. He was candid and truthful, and, after a few minutes, they unanimously voted, one by one as individuals, to support his course of action, despite its representing at least an additional year away from home.

In winning their allegiance, Amundsen had to openly discuss why he had chosen to withhold the truth from them. It was a speech that galvanized the team. Amundsen revealed his own personal risks and, in the same speech, expressed his well-founded belief that the team could achieve the new goal. Amundsen took everyone into his confidence on the plan. In addition, he announced arrangements to provide additional pay to team members choosing to accompany him on the South Polar attempt, as well as guarantees holding their jobs at home for the extended period of the new expedition. The team members could now choose to join him or accept a paid-return home. The new plan was to move fast and beat Scott to the Pole. Amundsen saw this success as their ticket to future resources for further exploration. If they succeeded, he believed that all of this secrecy and duplicity would be forgiven. If he failed, his reputation would be destroyed.

Now that Amundsen and his ship were cut off from the outside world and heading south, he put these worries out of his mind. There was work to be done, and Amundsen concentrated on the task at hand. The team's equipment had to be fit for every purpose and possibility. For example, during the ship's voyage, the team was constantly making customised improvements to the equipment. Adjusting all elements of equipment to conserve energy during the upcoming race was a theme in their efforts. Not just conserving food and raw material, but physical and mental energy as well. On board, there was not a moment to spare for relaxation. The project was in full swing and every possibility was attended to, not just once, but several times. Everyone had work to do and all of it focused on the goals and challenges that lay ahead.[19]

To the Pole: achieving the stretch target

Amundsen and his rival, Scott, both arrived in Antarctica in January, 1911. There was much preparation for both before the assault on the South Pole began. Before waiting out the winter months in total darkness, each team had to lay supply depots. Tensions ran high. Where were the competing parties? Would the South Pole reveal surprises? It was, after all, unknown territory. Two competitors were going head-to-head and time pressures mounted. After wintering at their bases, they both planned to begin their race in the 'spring' of the southern hemisphere, around October. Amundsen's team immediately set out to make camp and hunt seals. They

19 Huntford, op. cit., p. 245.

deployed a prefabricated Norwegian house that they brought with them, in order to have a touch of home through the winter. They also applied the lessons that Amundsen had learned from a lifetime of experience in Arctic exploration.

Managerial details behind building this virtuoso team

Amundsen's talent for leadership was reflected in the upbeat mood in the Norwegians' camp. Everyone continued to occupy themselves with tasks to improve equipment. The team was cohesive and full of purpose. Amundsen repeatedly emphasized that each improvement, and by extension every person's role, was of crucial importance. Bjaaland eventually reduced the weight of each sledge by up to 50 kilos while strengthening their frames; the boots for the trek were torn apart and re-sewn a total of four times; and the tents were dyed black with shoe polish to improve their visibility and retention of solar heat as well as sewn together to increase their internal warmth by the sharing of body heat.

While delegating these tasks, Amundsen strove to avoid the appearance of interfering with the mens' activities, preferring that each team member felt valued, trusted and autonomous. In an effort to maintain morale, he also made little occasions for his group to look forward to, such as brandy toddies every Saturday or weekly saunas; there were also prizes for weather prediction.[20]

---

20 Huntford, op. cit., pp. 366–73.

On a few trial runs for the supply-depot journeys, Amundsen demonstrated for everyone that his plan to combine dogs for transport with men accompanying on skis was a good one. It was simple and fast, capable of covering up to 30 miles per day. The dogs, of which there were approximately 200, were well-suited for the terrain and of the highest quality that existed. Their diet was so flexible that they could eat anything from seal meat to each other, and even their own excrement if necessary. They were also excellent psychological companions for his men, whose affections helped them to overcome the loneliness forced on them for the duration of the multi-year expedition.

Amundsen planned to travel an average of 20 miles per day on the race for the Pole, which set a concrete, realizable goal; between five and six hours was allotted for rest each day and one day in four could be set aside for rest in case of bad weather. The placement of supply depots was clearly marked and included far more food than their diets required. Taken together, there were wide margins of safety.[21]

During the winter, Amundsen's team worked. The Norwegian home was improved with three new subterranean rooms built into the ice for sewing, storage, laundry, a WC and carpentry workshop. Work on the sledges continued to make them lighter and lighter, in addition to building four new ones. The boots were found to be too small and were re-sewn. Packing crates were lightened, and 40,000 biscuits and supplies of powdered

21 Huntford, op. cit., pp. 290–95.

milk were stored so they could be retrieved without undoing the crates, a small but important innovation for the time. Plans were gone over again and again, frequently giving rise to discussions and more suggestions for small innovations. All in all, the team was kept busy, on a routine, and focused on their goal.

A number of uncertainties gnawed at Amundsen nonetheless. First, the presence of Scott's motor sledges greatly worried him: they represented the most significant unpredictable factor in the race. Second, while his choice of base camp shaved 120 miles from their path to and from the South Pole, the terrain was entirely unexplored, with the exception of the supply lines they had established. In particular, Amundsen had to find a path through the mountain ridges. These were riddled with potentially lethal crevasses and dead ends. Third, there was the simmering conflict with Johansen. He was now openly competing for psychological leadership of the expedition and his blunt manner grated on Amundsen. Virtually all of the other team members understood that, while confident in his methods, Amundsen was sensitive to challenges to his authority. They had learned that the best way to contest his judgments was to ask questions. This put Amundsen at ease to discuss them openly and rationally. Johansen ignored this. He argued abrasively and in the process damaged the harmony of the group. These worries pushed Amundsen to his first great mistake.[22]

22 Huntford, op. cit., pp. 374–76.

Leadership crisis and recovery

A big decision was when to start the run for the Pole as the spring weather approached. A successful fast start would be an enormous advantage to either team, but starting too early, and encountering late-winter storms, bitterly cold temperatures, and the darkness of the polar night, could be a fatal mistake, ending not only their hopes but perhaps their lives as well. In spite of preparation, this decision was one that had to be made on the spot, based on weather and a sense of the competitor's moves. Worried that Scott had superior technology, and driven by his dream to be there first, Amundsen rushed into a premature attempt at the Pole. He was forced back at the danger of losing the lives of both men and dogs.

Amundsen's premature start was a serious mistake in judgment. Knowing that a second place arrival at the Pole meant ruin – the Norwegian government had declined to support him when it learned of his change of plans – Amundsen had been anxious to take off as soon as possible. He decided to leave at the end of August, when by all measures it was far too early. Not only was it dangerously cold for the dogs at –40 degrees centigrade, which was compounded by a bitter head wind, but the nights were still extremely long. During their humiliating return, all order broke down in the final push as the men dashed on alone for the warmth of the winter hut. Those who had arrived waited, demoralized and worried that they faced defeat. Johansen, left behind without provisions, appears to have saved the life of a frost-bitten comrade and arrived at the hut in a brutal rage.[23] Amundsen's mistaken

23 Huntford, op. cit., pp. 390–92.

judgment – and the panicked retreat – exposed the hidden tensions within the group. At this point, the leadership of the expedition was in doubt. Amundsen had potentially lost the trust of his team. Johansen's challenge was an open call to mutiny. Other team members might have agreed with Johansen regarding Amundsen's decision to leave at such an early date. Still, they were stunned at the bitterness of Johansen's outburst, perhaps driven in part by his own feelings of a failed career. Amundsen knew something had to be done quickly or his men might refuse to follow him again.

Amundsen needed his men to follow him predominantly by choice earned through respect as a leader of professionals. That meant they had to understand his actions and agree with the course he chose. Though Johansen apparently regretted his outburst, it was the end of the 'splendid unity' that Amundsen had striven so hard to instill. Amundsen and Johansen were no longer on speaking terms. Amundsen also suspected that Johansen might sow further dissension during the next attempt to reach the Pole, which he deemed a threat to group survival.[24]

A leadership crisis was now full-blown. The expedition was in peril. The team was unraveling. Amundsen needed to quickly decide how to proceed. Without discussion, he immediately decided that Johansen and two other team members, who were openly embittered by the premature Pole attempt, would not be included in the next trip. They would explore the nearby Edward VII Island, with an uncharted interior. Enraged, Johansen demanded written

24 Huntford, op. cit., p. 393.

orders. Amundsen promptly delivered them. This reduced the Polar team to just five men. Amundsen interviewed each individually, requesting a renewed declaration of loyalty to him. Those who would go with him 'unreservedly accepted [his] leadership.'[25] In effect, Johansen and his sympathizers were permanently excluded from the inner circle and the final run to the Pole.

Achieving the stretch target

Amundsen embarked again at the end of October 1911. The morale of his chosen group remained high. They had learned a lot about their equipment during their winter respite, had improved nearly everything, and once again they had followed their leader's plan in clockwork order. Scott's team, on the other hand, was divided and not as confident as their resource advantage would suggest; the motor sledges had proven unreliable and would be left behind for lack of spare parts, while the horses were faltering in the cold and the dogs were left at base camp with Cecil Meares, a dog expert hired by Scott for his team. Among other duties, he was charged with acquiring the horses that Scott also brought on his expedition. That left man-hauling, which translated into eight hours of trudging through the snow each day to advance about 12 miles per day, or less than half the rate that Amundsen could achieve. On the other hand, Amundsen's route was completely uncharted and in fact turned out to be the most difficult of all the routes to the South Pole.[26]

25 Huntford, op. cit., pp. 395–96.
26 Huntford, op. cit., p. 431.

Amundsen's choice of march reveals much about the man and how he saw the leadership role. Amundsen knew that he had no 'touch' with the dogs and he chose not to have a dog team of his own. In addition, as the commander of the expedition, he needed to be able to move up and down the line, sometimes ahead of the dogs, but mostly behind, so that he could see what was going on. In many ways, Amundsen saw the role of leader as a very modest one: 'However hard you try, something is always going to fall off the sledge.' So, to be at the end of the line was the position of greatest responsibility. Amundsen felt that the glamour of being at the head of the line was less important than the value of being able to secure needed items that were at risk of loss.[27]

Amundsen's team quickly settled into a routine that included ample rest and relaxation. Learning from Amundsen's prior work with the Eskimos, they were kept fresh for their task and had plenty of energy reserves. In addition, their balanced diet ensured that they would not suffer vitamin deficiencies. Amundsen had allowed a full week to find a crossing, and they headed due south rather than seek a more circuitous route. Once, when Amundsen chose the wrong path, wasting an entire day, the team avoided all recrimination, in part because they had participated in this decision. Later, despite their affection for the animals, at the top of the mountain range they slaughtered many of their dogs, as planned, keeping only the best few for the remaining trek to the Pole. Throughout these tests, and in spite of his many anxieties,

27 Private conversation with Roland Huntford, September 2004, Lausanne, Switzerland.

Amundsen kept a level head, never pushing his men to exhaustion to save a few hours or days, but sticking to the pace they had agreed upon. On December 15, they reached the Pole, which felt like something of an anticlimax.[28] As Amundsen wrote:

> I had better be honest and say right out that I believe no human being has stood so diametrically opposed to the goal of his wishes . . . the North Pole had attracted me since the days of my childhood, and so I found myself on the South Pole. Can anything more perverse be conceived?[29]

Amundsen insisted that the entire team plant the flag together, sharing the historic moment equally. His attention then immediately shifted to returning safely and quickly to get his message out before Scott (who was 360 miles behind them and would not arrive at the Pole for another five weeks) had any chance to compromise their victory. They arrived back at base camp without incident.[30]

On January 17, 1912 Scott's team arrived at the Pole to find that Amundsen had beaten them. Upon turning back, Scott and his men heroically labored under the grim realization that their survival was at stake; finding each supply depot had become a race against starvation and frostbite. Because the horses had delayed the group's start, the weather was also 10 degrees colder than when Amundsen had passed through and was worsening rapidly as the Antarctic summer ended.[31] On the way back from the Pole, the first casualty of Scott's group was

---

28 Huntford, op. cit., pp. 466–69.
29 As cited in Huntford, op. cit., p. 469.
30 Huntford, op. cit., p. 470.
31 Huntford, op. cit., p. 491.

Lawrence Oates, a cavalry captain, whose gangrenous feet had become so painful that he could no longer continue. Silently, with great personal bravery, he crawled out of the tent to die in the cold with the brief comment: 'I am just going outside and may be some time.' The remaining group struggled forward for a few more days. Then they were overcome by a blizzard. Starving and exhausted, and suffering from scurvy and frostbite, the remainder of Scott's party lay in their sleeping bags to await their deaths, surviving for about nine days.[32]

Implications for leading virtuoso teams: Summary and Key Questions

Amundsen's ambition and vision were truly characteristic of a virtuoso team. He needed the most talented professionals – position by position – if he ever hoped to achieve his goals. What he understood and many contemporary managers seemingly fail to grasp, is that he needed the very best – only the best – talent obtainable to make his vision a reality. There is absolutely no point having a bold vision for change then stacking the odds against yourself by putting a team of average performers together. He settled for nothing less than the best. Managers leading or launching virtuoso teams need to settle for nothing less than the very best. Your virtuoso team must be a magnet for the very best talent you can possibly obtain, by attracting the very best from the very beginning.

Not only did Amundsen attract the very best, he also provided them the space they needed so that they could soar as individuals, but within a team context. He united them under a compelling common vision and goal. He provided the entire team with all the information needed to understand the nature of that goal and the plan to achieve it. Through discussions with each team member and in disseminating key information, Amundsen allowed each person on

32 Huntford, op. cit., pp. 523–39.

the team to know their role in achieving its vision for success. This was essential for each individual to exhibit their full potential while assisting the team in reaching its collective goals. Your virtuoso teams can only soar if they follow these prescriptions for excellence so carefully put into place by Amundsen. It is essential that in your organization's virtuoso teams, leadership sets a goal and then allows the expert team members to figure out the best way to reach that vision. Unlike many other teams in your firm, who are involved in the day-to-day activities of the business, virtuoso teams are comprised of true knowledge professionals. They, in most instances, know more about their own skill domain than does the leader. Yet time and time again, we see leaders attempt to tell such experts how to do their job. There is nothing more counterproductive. Amundsen understood full well that building a vision, ensuring absolute role clarity, and then getting out of his people's way once that vision was fully understood, was essential to getting the most out of the professionals on his team.

All of this means that the leader of a virtuoso team must be a relentless and consummate communicator. You've got to know what talent really is, and benchmark outside of your organization continually, in order to be assured that you have the very best. The Amundsen experience shows that along with great talent, it is ideas and know-how that make the difference between success and failure. Frequently, in fact, as Amundsen's experience further shows, it is often knowledge from outside the team's normal world that provides the key difference. Creating a strategy for idea acquisition is a first step for any leader. That strategy should include a clear understanding of where the best ideas are likely to reside; what personal network needs to be built to tap into those ideas and experiences; and where inside and outside the organization you as a leader should be spending time, with a dedicated focus on learning and acquiring the very best insights.

Finally, we turn to the power of details and execution. Amundsen illustrates the vital importance of leaving no stone unturned in understanding what must be done to reach the overall vision. In addition, as important as the details are, it is what is done with those plans that matters most. Every team member knew their and everyone else's role, enabling each virtuoso to gauge best how their expertise should and would contribute to achieving the vision. Such basic understanding is vital if improvisation is required and the plans are changing. A key requirement of a leader is to prepare their virtuoso team for the unforeseen, and by building a deep knowledge domain across the group about each professional's role and the overall planning details, the unexpected can be dealt with much more effectively.

These are but a few of the virtuoso team lessons that emerge from Amundsen's brilliant achievement. As you prepare for your organization's next big project, it is worth spending some time asking and answering some questions aimed at making your efforts to drive big change likely to succeed:

1 Have you selected the very best professionals for your virtuoso team? Position by position?

2 As a leader, are you giving your most talented people the space they need to soar? The space they need to build their own community and culture free and clear of the leader's influence and control?

3 Are you as a leader providing your virtuosos with a vision for what must be achieved and then getting out of the way? Or are you trying to tell them how to do their job?

4 What is your commitment to learning as a leader? Are you an effective and energetic student of the knowledge that you need, bringing in know-how, ideas, or experiences from outside the team and infusing those assets into the team to help them accomplish great things?

5 Is your planning thorough and aimed at every detail of your team's endeavor? Are you communicating your plans effectively to the team, making sure they can individually see their role in the overall scheme of what has to be done, and how they influence reaching the vision everyone is shooting for?

Notes

This chapter was inspired by the work of Roland Huntford in his book *Scott and Amundsen: The Last Place on Earth*. Most of what appears in this chapter was guided by Professor Huntford's research, as well as several private conversations that we have been privileged to have with him. There are several other works, which the authors found extremely helpful in understanding Amundsen's team. These include:

Amundsen, Roald. *The South Pole*. Edinburgh: Birlinn, 2002.

Fiennes, Sir Ralph. *Race to the Pole*. New York: Hyperion, 2004.

Jones, Max. *The Last Great Quest*. Oxford: Oxford University Press, 2003.

Solomon, Susan. *The Coldest March*. New Haven: Yale University Press, 2001.

6

Deliver great results, week by week

Balancing freedom with direction under Sid Caesar's leadership

He had total control, but we had total freedom.[1]
Larry Gelbart

Throughout this book, we've seen numerous examples of virtuoso teams being larger than life, characterized by an almost incandescent creative energy that sets them apart from most of the project teams that we see in daily work. The legacy of these teams can be found in the discontinuous changes that they effect on their 'industries:' new approaches to popular theater (*West Side Story*), the birth of the 'atomic age' (the Manhattan Project), etc. They also, however, mark their members for life, as members of a group that for one brief moment rose above the rest to change their world. One such team that has forever been referred to as 'The Writers' Group' is the team that wrote for comedian Sid Caesar. Including Mel Brooks, Woody Allen, Neil Simon and Carl Reiner, among others, this team has a legendary quality about its members and its accomplishments – one commentator went so far as to call it: 'the greatest writing room

1 Gelbart, Larry, quoted in a transcript of 'Caesar's Hour Revisited,' a seminar of the Writers' Guild of America (west), broadcast on PBS, 1996.
www.nytimes.com/books/first/g/gelbart-laughing.htmls

since William Shakespeare wrote alone.'[2] What we'll see in this chapter, however, is that from a managerial viewpoint this team was more than just a group of brilliant people; it was a well-led, fully integrated team.

In this chapter, look for the balance between 'freedom' and 'direction' that characterizes the way the virtuoso team worked, and which was the hallmark of Sid Caesar's leadership style. Although frequently portrayed as chaotic, it was anything but that. Neither anarchic nor democratic, this was a team of strong egos that nonetheless had a strong central leader. His decisions, once arrived at, became the rule, yet no one felt left out of the 'governance' process. Indeed, the physical nature of the workspace (basically, one crowded room), the transparency of communications, and the direct conversations fostered team success.

Virtuoso teams and their leaders are well-tuned ideas machines. With Caesar's writers, the process by which ideas were generated, considered and either accepted or rejected, all resulted in everyone feeling that they were 'involved' in everything that happened within the team. Key to this case, as well, is how the central role of the leader is so well illustrated by Sid Caesar. This was a group of ambitious and talented virtuoso performers. The way that Caesar gave them direction, and then immediately stayed out of their way, and finally prototyped their ideas, was an extremely demanding, but effective, leadership role to play.

Finally, it was a team where competition among new ideas, rather than competition between idea-creators, was the norm. Caesar, as leader, set up a marketplace for ideas, another hallmark of virtuoso teams. In this market, ideas are created and then chosen and survive only based on their contribution to the team's goals, rather than on the power or position of the individual coming up

2 Claster, Bob, quoted in 'Caesar's Hour Revisited,' *Written By*, March 1996.
www.wga.org

with the idea. In this virtuoso team, we'll also learn about a group that transformed its industry by deliberately stretching its customers – giving them a product that 'raised' them rather than 'lowered' them – and stretched itself in the process. Their vision was clear, understood and ennobling; Caesar wanted to change how the market defined comedy, and he and his team did just that. The team, each and every member, knew who they were and what they were trying to accomplish. They had a leader who licensed them to create *big change,* and who trusted them to deliver. And, of course, his was a team that as a result of all of this, was legendary in their accomplishments.

Fast product creation: every week half a Broadway show

Creating great comedy is not just about funny people doing strange things. Many of their goals are strikingly similar to those of visionary business-people, scientists, and designers: they want to achieve something revolutionary – a fundamental recasting of their field – and they want to wow their customers, peers, or audience; not least, they want to advance their careers and, by extension, make money. That is why *Your Show of Shows*, a 1950s American television comedy series starring Sid Caesar, offers fascinating lessons on one of the most successful virtuoso teams we have studied. Not only did Caesar's writers challenge the standard practices of a new and rapidly-evolving industry, but they did so consistently over a number of years with seemingly impossible deadlines every week.

How did they do it? In a nutshell, Sid Caesar put a group of phenomenally talented writers into an empty room and let them be themselves while offering subtle, and occasionally brutal, hints at how they should work together rather than directing (or 'micro-managing') them. Caesar nurtured an environment to spawn creativity. In what we regard as a quintessential virtuoso team, the group included Mel Brooks, who went on to create a number of pioneering comedies, and Woody Allen who also got his big break as part of Caesar's team and later came into his own as an Oscar-winning scriptwriter and filmmaker. In addition, there was the celebrated producer, director, writer, and comedian Carl Reiner (creator of *The Dick Van Dyke Show*), as well as Larry Gelbart, who created the M*A*S*H television series and the Broadway play *City of Angels*. Finally, prior to becoming one of America's most successful Broadway playwrights, Neil Simon began his writing career on the Caesar show. In spite of their huge egos and now-famous eccentricities, this group worked as a team, sometimes offering solo performances, but always as a part of something bigger.

The vision: giving the customer more, not less

A new technology often creates the opportunity for revolutionary innovation. The search for content to suit the new *carrier* technology of television began by employing traditional entertainment offerings to find a product that audiences would be comfortable with. Comedy was a natural offering, and almost as naturally, the earliest television comedies tended to be pure slapstick. One comedian, Sid Caesar, stood out from most others of the time not only as a student of his craft but also because of his thoughts regarding the art and message of comedy. In his autobiography, *Where Have I Been?*, he recalls wondering:

> '[W]hy did so much comedy of that day depend on the degradation of another human being? Why did most of the laughs seem to come from throwing a pie in someone's face or squirting him with a seltzer bottle? Certainly there was another way.'[3]

In spite of the demonstrated market for that crude kind of slapstick, Caesar wanted to do something more, to tickle the intelligence of the growing television audience; in his words, to dare, 'to satirize modern painting, psychiatry, movie epics, advertising, and other themes not commonly treated on television.'[4]

Caesar pursued this ennobling vision of the customer with a kindred spirit, the producer and director Max Liebman, whose vision was similar to that of Caesar. In addition to his desire to succeed in the extraordinarily competitive industry of entertainment television, he too wanted to create something original in the world of music and comedy, a show that did not simply repeat the gags of the past, but one which would be remembered for the statements it made, as well as for the laughs it elicited. The audience, Liebman believed, was ready to be stretched to a higher level of satire:

> One thing we take for granted on our show is that the mass audience we're trying to reach isn't a dumb one, it has a high quota of intelligence, and there's no need to

3 Caesar, Sid. *Where Have I Been?* New York: Crown, 1982, p. 31.
4 Sennett, Ted. *Your Show of Shows.* New York: Macmillan, 1977, p. 12.

play down to it. That is why we try to maintain a mature approach. We strive for adult entertainment, without compromise, and believe that the audience will understand it.[5]

Liebman's concept of sophistication included bringing opera and dance into the American home. He explained it:

I don't mean the kind of sophistication which is over the heads of the audience. I'm referring to sophistication tempered by a sense of showmanship that brings the audience something they may not be as familiar with as they were in vaudeville, but something within their grasp to comprehend and appreciate.[6]

This vision had deep roots in the American vaudeville stage, of course, which provided much of the initial inspiration for television comedy programming. For more than 20 years prior to the launch of these shows, Liebman had been preparing for this moment, starting in Pennsylvania's Pocono Mountains – a major vacation spot in the mid-20th century – and then moving on to nightclubs, vaudeville, and finally Broadway. Liebman had studied the techniques to reach a mass audience and over the years forged a number of influential contacts. With the invention of the medium of television, Liebman sensed that his opportunity had come.[7] As 'the expert,' Liebman was prepared to produce and direct this new style of variety show on television.

5 Liebman, Max, quoted in a 1950 Boston newspaper interview, in Sennett, op. cit., p. 6.
6 Sennett, op. cit., p. 10.
7 Sennett, op. cit., pp. 11–14.

Liebman's style was that of a quiet, behind-the-scenes player. Neil Simon put it this way:

> He wasn't funny. He was the producer. He was wonderful. I think he had a Viennese background, and he had a wonderful sense of taste that imbued all of us, so we didn't go over the edge. Max was quite brilliant but . . . [he's] sort of the invisible man. But I think he liked being the invisible man.[8]

In the early 1950s, the dream of Caesar and Liebman was revolutionary and extremely risky. The prevailing view of television executives of the American mass audience was one of little regard for its intelligence, willingness to learn, or capacity to appreciate sophisticated themes. To go forward, Liebman had to build political support within the managerial hierarchy of the television network (NBC) that would carry the show, as well as with the original commercial sponsors, including the television manufacturer Admiral. A critically important believer in the concept was Pat Weaver, an NBC vice-president. In addition to the initial approval and political cover that he provided for this innovation, he agreed to absorb the costs of the prototype without sponsorship, which was unprecedented at that time. In doing this, he typified the audacity that characterized the entire project, though he was never a formal member of the team. In Sid Caesar's words: 'He was willing to experiment [along] with you.'[9] At a reunion of 'Caesar's Writers' in 1996, Caesar reminisces about Weaver:

---

8 Simon, Neil, quoted in an interview about *Laughter on the 23rd Floor*, *Entertainment Tonight*, May 24, 2001. **www.etonline.com/television/a3410.htm**
9 Caesar, Sid. 'For the Record.' Interview with Dan Pasternack, March 14, 1997. **www.emmys.com/foundation/archive/vault/win1999/page3.html**

And I must say, Pat Weaver put his neck on the block because . . . the first four shows were not sponsored. [But] Weaver said, 'I want it on.' I remember the cost of the show – with all the writers, all the actors, all the musicians, all the dancers, all the costumes, all the scenery – was $19,000 a week for an hour. Nineteen thousand dollars a week, and they were shaking in their boots and going, 'Let's go.'[10]

Act 1: achieving the vision

And so the *Admiral Broadway Revue* was born. It was Sid Caesar's first show. To the surprise of many it was an immediate success and soon became one of the most popular shows in television history; without tele-visions at home, some people were reported to drive 50 miles to see it on someone else's. Liebman received support for his radical ideas in fan letters, which, 'mention[ed] how much they had enjoyed and appreciated the operas and ballets they had never seen before. It was not beyond their ken. The show was performed in a manner that didn't patronize these people.'[11] In retrospect, the *Revue* was the first step in Liebman's becoming 'a major influence on American taste in the fifties.'[12]

The *Revue* was also innovative for pioneering a number of practices that were to become industry standards, including: the hiring of a permanent cast and staff of writers, set designers, choreographers and a ballet corps; scenery that was built, stored, repainted, and reused; the use of lighting to convey mood and style, rather than

10 Caesar, Sid, quoted in 'Caesar's Hour Revisited,' op. cit.
11 Sennett, op. cit., p. 10.
12 Cunard, David. Review of *Lady in the Dark*, March 24, 1997.
www.londontheater.co.uk/londontheater/castrecordings/ladyinthedark.htm

merely to illuminate; the use of a theater designed
expressly for television, the International Theater at
Columbus Circle in New York City; live performances in a
Broadway theater in front of a full audience; and
simultaneous broadcasts on the major networks, allowing
it to be seen over the combined East-West Dumont
network and on NBC stations in 31 cities.[13]

Paradoxically, the ultimate measure of the *Admiral
Broadway Revue's* success was the show's cancellation.
After a single season, Admiral withdrew its support. The
reason, according to Admiral's management, was that the
demand for their product – television sets – had grown so
spectacularly during the show's initial season that the
company no longer had discretionary money for
advertising and sponsorship. To meet the increased
demand for television sets, the company had to invest all
its available capital in its manufacturing capacity. In a
meeting between Caesar and Ross Siragusa, Admiral's
president, Caesar was given notice in the following terms:

> You're wondering, I'm sure, why we canceled such a
> popular show . . . At the time we took on the show, we
> were selling maybe five hundred to eight hundred
> [television] sets a week. After the third week of the show,
> we had orders for five thousand sets a week. It's still
> going up now. As of today, we have orders for ten
> thousand sets a week . . . We faced a difficult decision.
> We have just so much money, and we had to make up our
> minds whether to put it into capital investment, or to
> keep putting it into the show. Honestly, we had to put the
> money into capital investment and retool – just to keep
> up with the orders.[14]

13 Sennett, op. cit., p. 13.
14 Siragusa, Ross, quoted in Caesar, Sid. *Where Have I Been?* New York:
Crown, 1982, pp. 89–90.

In spite of this setback, Liebman and Caesar had a team in place and were ready for their next venture, *Your Show of Shows*.

The dream team

With a new show in the planning, Max Liebman and Sid Caesar put together a first-rate team of comedy writers. The pressure on the team would be enormous: not only would they have to meet the highest standards of sophistication, quality, and originality, but every week Caesar and the other performers would have to entertain a live audience during a 90-minute, nationwide broadcast. Caesar describes it as putting on half of a Broadway play – new – each week, and doing it in real time:

> Live, the adrenaline flows through you; you have to make an impression. There's just one shot to come up with the top performance. You get a rhythm going and the audience going, and you can play with that.[15]

In addition to the stress, there was a contagious excitement for the team in this challenge. According to Max Liebman:

> Any Broadway actor will tell you that he's in the business because it's exciting as well as challenging. And it is! But look what we have on television. Whereas it takes months and months to put on a two-hour revue on Broadway, we do an original one-hour show, with singing, dancing, and comedy – in one week. Theater die-hards speak of the thrill of opening night. Hell, we have one every week![16]

15 Caesar, Sid. 'Hail Caesar.' Interview with David Rensin. **www.aarp.org/mmaturity/nov_dec00/cameo.html**
16 Sennett, op. cit., p. 18.

Critics and viewers alike were awestruck at the complexity and demands of the weekly production. 'How is it possible,' Liebman was frequently asked, 'to turn out a well-received, award-winning, and yet still creative and fresh show of 90 minutes, every week?' His answer:

> There *is* no formula, except we have the best talent available in each capacity. What really counts is taste, style, experience, and, above all, showmanship.[17]

It was the writers who stood at the heart of the challenge in the various television series that were called 'Caesar's Empire.' Acclaimed as 'the greatest writing staff in the history of television,'[18] it was, according to Caesar, '. . . a writing staff that was a dream team . . . You can't explain it. . . . It's a gathering of great minds . . . You sit in the room with the giants – I mean, these were real giant writers.'[19] Larry Gelbart compares them to a jazz ensemble:

> Except for the fact that we were all white and Jewish, we felt like we were the Duke Ellington band. We had this great sound together. Everybody is valuable when you're writing that way.[20]

Although Caesar was always present during both concept and script development as an intimate collaborator, he never actually wrote anything; in other words, while he was involved in every detail, he knew that he could not do everything. His initial team included Lucille Kallen

---

17 Sennett, op. cit., p. 23. Liebman was an expert 'talent scout' and among his credits is the way he encouraged Jerome Robbins (part of the team that created *West Side Story*) to choreograph some small reviews in the late 1930s.
www.androsdance.tripod.com/biographies/robbins_jerome.htm
18 Tobias, Patricia Eliot. 'Great Caesar's Scripts.' *Written By*, May 2001.
www.wga.org
19 Caesar, Sid. 'For the Record,' op. cit.
20 Gelbart, Larry, quoted in a transcript of 'Caesar's Hour Revisited,' op. cit.

and Mel Tolkin (later one of the key writers in the extraordinarily influential 1970s tele-vision series *All in the Family*); they had worked for many years with Liebman and were superb lyricists and composers, as well as comedy writers. Tony Webster was also an early writer, who had previously worked for the hit comedians Bob and Ray. Mel Brooks and, later, Carl Reiner, Neil Simon, and Woody Allen were added to the team.

The team was hand-picked by the leaders, Caesar and Liebman, often with lightning quick judgment. With the intimate involvement of the two leaders rather than through a human resources department, these choices were entirely personal and intuitive. As writer Howard Morris recalled:

> In 1949 I was looking for a job in New York when I ran into an old friend. He said, 'Go across the street to that building, go to the top floor, and ask for Max Liebman. He's producing a television show for a guy named Sid Caesar.' On the fourth floor I heard some singing coming from one of the rooms and went in. Four guys were carrying a lady around. I didn't know it at the time but she was Imogene Coca. I asked for Mr. Liebman. Someone said, 'He's in the girls' locker room, writing.' I went down and knocked on the door, and he introduced me to a hulk in the corner – Sid Caesar. Sid and I read a scene together, and at the end of it he lifted me up by the lapels. Sid looked over at Max and said, 'Him . . . get.' And that's how I was hired – because he could lift me.[21]

Not surprisingly, this great talent was accompanied by equally great egos: there were strident clashes of personality and tempers were often badly frayed. For

21 Caesar, Sid. 'Hail Caesar,' op. cit.

example, writer Mel Brooks frequently rubbed Liebman
the wrong way. According to Brooks:

> The truth was that Max Liebman was not exactly thrilled
> to have me around. When he saw me, he assessed my
> character and personality immediately. He was absolutely
> right. He saw an arrogant, obnoxious little shithead who
> thought he knew everything and had patience for nothing
> but his own thoughts. But Sid convinced him and
> prevailed, eventually.[22]

Not only did the writers know that they were part of an
elite team, they were proud of it. According to Woody
Allen: 'Sid Caesar was the show to which all comedy
writers aspired. It was the place you wanted to be.'[23] Mel
Brooks, who wrote for the whole run of the two main
Caesar shows, put it this way:

> I should have been impressed, but I wasn't, because I was
> a cocky kid, filled with hubris and this marvelous ego.
> And I thought I was God's gift to creative writing . . . and
> it turned out I was.[24]

Act 2: accelerating creativity

Packed into a small and intimate space, Caesar's team
faced a series of extremely rigid deadlines. The
environment was honest and open, a kind of 'creative
chaos,' in which the writers had the freedom to do what
they did best. According to team member Larry Gelbart: 'It
was very much like going to work every day of the week
inside a Marx Brothers movie.'[25] Nonetheless, while often

22 Brooks, Mel, quoted in 'Caesar's Hour Revisited,' op. cit.
23 Tobias, op. cit.
24 Ibid.
25 Gelbart, Larry, quoted in a transcript of 'Caesar's Hour Revisited,' op. cit.

they were having fun, they were all aware that they were there to succeed and make money.

Beginning on Monday, each week the writer's group worked toward a deadline of the following Saturday evening, when the show was broadcast live to up to 20 million television viewers. The writers typically began the new week's work either alone or in pairs, depending upon their assignments. They later came together in a small 'writing room' to share and compare the ideas that they had come up with. Ideas, situations, and lines would be tossed back and forth, and while most would be rejected, a choice few would be accepted and pursued. The pace was dizzying, yet everyone stayed focused: they knew, in such a volatile industry as television, that their careers were on the line every week; there wasn't time to sulk or stay angry. As one of Neil Simon's characters puts it in the play *Laughter on the 23rd Floor*, which was based on the story of Caesar's writers: 'In this room? I can't afford [to be upset]. Funny is money! . . . In that room great comedy was born.'[26] Nanette Fabray (one of Caesar's female leads) describes the atmosphere: 'Everybody spoke at the top of their lungs. It was smoke up to here – everybody smoked – and food! There were piles of food on the tables.'[27]

While big egos there certainly were, Caesar's writers were able to strike a balance that allowed them to work together, somewhere in the uncomfortable area between collaboration and competition. A snippet of a

26 Simon, Neil. *Laughter on the 23rd Floor.* New York: Random House, 1995, p. 68.
27 Tobias, op. cit.

conversation between Sid Caesar, Carl Reiner and Larry
Gelbart illustrates this point:

> CAESAR: . . . it was phenomenal . . . to sit . . . and listen
> to the mayhem that was going back and forth, and
> electricity and hate.
>
> REINER: We call it competition. Competition.
>
> LARRY GELBART: We call it 'collaboration.'[28]

In addition, their working space had a great deal of
personality, which operated both to encourage the growth
of a group identity and, with its comfort and familiarity, to
facilitate their work: memories were etched into the space,
as was the learning that was constantly going on. People
could be themselves there, almost as if it were a second
home. Neil Simon vividly describes the physical space
they worked in for *Laughter on the 23rd Floor*:

> This is the Writers' Room. It is actually two rooms made
> into one large room by breaking down the wall that
> separated them. We can still see where the molding has
> stopped between the two rooms.
>
> The room is divided into two spaces. On Stage Left is
> where the actual writing takes place. There is a metal-top
> desk with a typewriter on it and a swivel chair behind it.
> A large leather sofa is to the left of the desk. On the
> opposite side of the desk and facing it, there is a large,
> comfortable sitting chair. This belongs to [Sid Caesar].
> Around this grouping are chairs of assorted kinds, room
> enough for eight people to sit down.
>
> The other side of the room, at Stage Right, is more of a
> lounging area. There is a table against the wall with a

28 Caesar, Sid, Reiner, Carl, and Gelbart, Larry, quoted in 'Caesar's Hour
Revisited,' op. cit.

coffeemaker on it, in which coffee is now perking. There are paper cups, and a few regular coffee mugs for the veteran writers. Also on the table is an assortment of fresh bagels, rolls and sliced pound cake, and Danish [pastries].

There is a small desk in this area with two chairs on either side and a telephone on top.

There is also a corkboard on the wall to which index cards are tacked to denote the sketches that are being written. There are also piles of magazines, dictionaries, and thesauri about. There are also two doors, one on each side of the room. Also, there are Emmys and other awards on the shelves . . .

The[re are] two holes in the wall left by Sid [and which] are both now framed in silver. [The silver frames and accompanying plaques were from Tiffany's. One hole was when Sid punched the wall after Senator Joseph McCarthy called General George Marshall 'a communist,' and the other was when he punched the wall after learning that NBC was going to send 'an observer' to observe the management of the show.] There are also two additional holes [for Julius and Ethel Rosenberg, the executed atomic 'spies'] on another place on the wall. These have simple black frames, no plaques.[29]

Strong leadership drives the action

Throughout the writing sessions, the focal point was the explosive Sid Caesar. He ran the writing sessions with perfection and speed, sometimes with the control of a very heavy hand. While there was freedom within which the writers could inject ideas and criticisms, it was not democratic nor was it consensus-based. In Larry Gelbart's words:

29 Simon, op. cit., pp. 3 and 63.

When he approved of a line as it was pitched by one of us, Caesar would nod subtly at Mike, in the manner of someone at an auction. Often it would be sharpened by someone else the minute the line took flight, and Mike, complying with the nod, would commit the new and improved line to paper.[30]

(Mike was Michael Stewart, a young man who served as a typist-editor-amanuensis, capturing the nonstop, raucous pitching of jokes and ideas. An invaluable aide, he was also a bright student of comedy, going on, post-Caesar, to write the books for Broadway hits such as *Bye Bye Birdie, Hello, Dolly!* and *42nd Street*.)

Caesar's method was to demand a succession of prototype sketches, always pushing for improvement and refinement. As Danny Simon recalls: 'I remember Max read one of the spots we wrote. He says, "This is good. This is one of the best spots I've ever read. Now rewrite it."'[31] In the maelstrom of brainstorming and joking, ownership of the ideas was difficult to pinpoint. Rather than deter members from putting their all into the effort, this created a sense of mutual respect and unity in the group, of belonging to something bigger than just oneself. The members of the team trusted each other to be their best, to pursue excellence. Max Liebman describes the process this way:

> An idea tentatively tossed into the air can be fatally impaled in mid-flight by a grunt from Caesar, or can soar up on his pleased grin and return to earth, shaped into a story, peopled and costumed. Let Miss Coco [the show's first female lead] suggest that there ought to be a skit

---

30 Gelbart, Larry, quoted in a transcript of 'Caesar's Hour Revisited,' op. cit.
31 Simon, Danny, quoted in 'Caesar's Hour Revisited,' op. cit.

about a couple on a bus, and that afternoon it is in rehearsal. Here is the strength I counted on at the outset, this unity of understanding, and the easy interchange of comedy values. We are richer nowhere than in our department of comedy, nor speedier.[32]

The Friday morning dry-run for the next evening's show was, Liebman continues, 'usually without dismaying incident . . . Sometimes, but not often, we may find a number considered irresistible all week is not only resistible but downright bad. This produces a major crisis, which is promptly referred to the writers who specialize in crises.'[33] Continuous writing and rewriting ensued at breakneck pace. As Mel Brooks remembers, 'We'd write a sketch in 35 to 40 minutes if we were stuck. We'd get a premise, and we'd bang it out. We had very talented guys.'[34] He elaborates:

Everyone pitched lines at Sid. Jokes would be changed 50 times. We'd take an eight-minute sketch and rewrite it in eight minutes. Then Sid and Coco and Reiner and Morris [the actors who would ultimately have to present the skit] would relearn it from scratch. On Saturday night, it had its first and only test – before 20 million people.[35]

But by that time, of course, it was no longer *untested*, having gone through countless rewrites in various forms.

Team trust and physical intimacy are the glue

The sense of intimacy and trust meant that the group did not feel the need to spend energy on politeness or harmony, which by unspoken agreement they seemed to

32 Liebman, Max, quoted in Sennett, op. cit., p. 25.
33 Sennett, op. cit., p. 28.
34 Tobias, op. cit.
35 Sennett, op. cit., p. 26.

believe would hinder the flow of ideas. In the common room with its frenetic pace, tempers flared and nerves were often jangled, but it remained exhilarating. Larry Gelbart remembers the average day beginning as: 'First we said 'Good morning.' That was the last purely social moment of the day.'[36] As Lucille Kallen described it:

> To command attention, I'd have to stand on a desk and wave my red sweater. Sid boomed, Tolkin intoned, Reiner trumpeted, and Brooks, well, Mel imitated everything from a rabbinical student to the white whale of Moby Dick thrashing about on the floor with six harpoons sticking in his back. Let's say that gentility was never a noticeable part of our working lives. Max Liebman was fond of quoting: 'From a polite conference, comes a polite movie.'[37]

Confrontation was not unusual within the team, and Mel Tolkin talks about what he called 'good creative anger.'[38] How far did it go? Mel Brooks gives this response in a *Playboy* interview:

> BRAD DARRACH: Is it true that everybody hated you on *Your Show of Shows*?
>
> MEL BROOKS: Everybody hated everybody. We robbed from the rich and kept everything.[39]

Although the writers were competitive, credit for a joke or a line was hard to identify or claim. In 1996, at a reunion of the Writers Group, Bob Claster asked a key question:

> CLASTER: How competitive was the atmosphere in the room, with you guys?

---

36 Gelbart, Larry, quoted in a transcript of 'Caesar's Hour Revisited,' op. cit.
37 Sennett, op. cit., p. 25.
38 Tolkin, Mel, quoted in Caesar, Sid. *Where Have I Been?*, op. cit., p. 145.
39 *Playboy* interview, 1975. **www.uahc.org/rjmag/1101ak.html**

BROOKS: Not at all! [All protest.] No, we loved each other!

BELKIN: I think that it should be pointed out, this was gang writing with 12 people in the room . . .

CLASTER: How carefully did you guys monitor how much of your individual material, if any . . . Was there ego involved?

REINER: No, not a bit. No.

NEIL SIMON: I went home to watch the shows and I laughed and laughed, and my wife says, 'That's your joke, isn't it?' And I said, 'I dunno.' We never knew. They all came so fast.

GELBART: But it wasn't ego-less. You can't do this without an ego.

REINER: The only thing people took credit for are the things they fought hard for. They fought hard and people fought against them, and if they got them in and it worked, fine. If it didn't work, they were embarrassed.

GELBART: Two minutes later you forgot they were yours.

TOLKIN: For instance, some guy may just hit an idea, a notion . . . And 10 jokes come out of that line. You know, you make a basic joke . . . and then you make variations. So who wrote the joke?

GELBART: The miracle was that, ultimately, there was some kind of structure, because we were throwing lines.

BROOKS: We were like a World Series ball club. We were all good hitters, good fielders, all good. And if we won the championship, let it be Larry Gelbart's home run. We won.[40]

---

40 'Caesar's Hour Revisited,' op. cit.

The open and intimate atmosphere also inspired the exchange of knowledge. According to Carl Reiner, 'It was like a college. Everybody learning from everybody else. It was absolutely amazing.'[41] Nonetheless, if a writer was not aggressively extroverted, the transmission of ideas remained a challenge. Caesar describes it this way:

> There was so much screaming and yelling in the writers' room that a shy, soft-spoken man didn't have a chance of getting his ideas across. Woody Allen and Neil Simon [Doc] both solved this problem by latching onto someone with a very loud mouth as a transmitter of their ideas. Carl Reiner, for example, was Doc's spokesman. Doc always sat next to Carl, and whenever I'd see him lean over and whisper something in Carl's ear, I'd say to myself, 'Aha, Doc has an idea.' Then Carl would get up and bellow, louder than anyone else, 'Doc's got an idea.' Still shouting, he would tell the idea.[42]

Virtuoso teams as a crucible for leadership development

For virtually everyone involved, membership in the writer's group was a crucible, that is, a vital, life-changing experience that served as preparation and underpinning for the rest of their careers. As writers, their opinions are best expressed in their own words. According to Lucille Kallen: 'It was a lot of fun. Can you imagine being young and single and at the top of the heap and writing for guest stars like Rex Harrison?' As Tony Webster saw it: 'For me, and I'm sure for all the other people, it was really exciting. The people were all talented and it was a perfect example

41 Ibid.
42 Caesar, Sid, *Where Have I Been?*, op. cit., p. 146.

of everyone contributing. It was a case of all the right people being in the right place at the same time. All very bright and talented.' Added Mel Tolkin: 'We were too young to know it's impossible . . . The biggest miracle was the combination of people. It was quite accidental, like any miracle. I think if it was one writer different, it wouldn't have been the same show.'[43] Carl Reiner remarks: 'We didn't know it was hard. It's like a bird. If he knew what he was doing, he would fall.'[44] 'We didn't know we couldn't do it,' says Mel Brooks, 'so we did it.'[45] Says Larry Gelbart: 'What helped us all a great deal was the fact that we were all young and largely unfamiliar with the word 'can't.' We took it as a matter of course that we would assemble at the start of every week to write a new, one-hour comedy/variety show, with the accent on comedy.'[46] Gelbart continues: 'I mean, it was a joy . . . I mean, this was a real treat for all of us. I don't think anyone has ever duplicated that experience among us.'[47] Perhaps, however, Neil Simon sums it up best: 'I also think that none of us who have gone on to do other things, could have done them without going through this show.'[48]

A virtuoso leader takes center stage

At the center of these shows were the multifaceted talents of Sid Caesar. As *Los Angeles Times* television critic Howard Rosenberg writes: 'Caesar would be on any short

43 Sennett, op. cit., p. 26.
44 Reiner, Carl, quoted in **www.emmys.com/whatwedo/halloffame/reiner.htm**
45 Tobias, op. cit.
46 Gelbart, Larry, quoted in a transcript of 'Caesar's Hour Revisited,' op. cit.
47 Gelbart, Larry, quoted in 'Caesar's Hour Revisited,' op. cit.
48 Simon, Neil, quoted in 'Caesar's Hour Revisited,' op. cit.

list of nominees for the most creative comic artist ever to work on TV.'[49] Liebman had recognized Caesar's promise well before the *Admiral Broadway Revue* and had brought him in along with the other talents assembled to create both the *Admiral Broadway Revue* and *Your Show of Shows*. But he also recognized that Caesar's talent demanded a solo performance style:

> He wanted to do things only the way he could, and this is the drive that governs any artist, any creative person. A painter wants to paint in his own way, and that's why so many are recognized by what they paint. That's why distinctive musicians, composers, and writers want to be recognized by that personal thing they bring to their work that nobody else does. And I used to say that Caesar insisted on instinctively Caesarizing his material. His material was sifted through a sieve that was truly personal. No matter how it went in, it came out as Caesar.[50]

Caesar was also the team's *leader*, attracting people to work for him personally rather than for the company and, like Liebman, an expert at spotting talent. He was consistently able to find and then enlist the best people to work for him. Years later, Brooks describes his allegiance:

> I didn't belong to the show, I didn't belong to Max Liebman. I belonged to Sid. And Sid could call me, night or day, and sometimes he'd wake me up at 3:30 in the morning and say, 'Mel? Sid. Need a joke.'[51]

Neil Simon, speaking through the character Lucas Brickman in *Laughter on the 23rd Floor*, says: 'I like [Sid] a lot. Mostly because he treated his writers with respect.'[52]

49 Rosenberg, Howard, quoted in **www.freespace.virgin.net/steve.hulse/sidc.htm**
50 Sennett, op. cit., p. 37.
51 Brooks, Mel, quoted in 'Caesar's Hour Revisited,' op. cit.
52 Simon, op. cit., p. 4.

According to Larry Gelbart: '. . . when it came to putting together a writing staff for his own venture, Sid Caesar was all method and no madness. Hence, Mel Tolkin. Hence, Mel Brooks.'[53] He was also the person who set the tone for freedom within the context of group discipline. While chaotic to the outside observer – and often to members of the group and to NBC management – there was a sharp focus to what they were doing, with clear boundaries and goals, all of which were not rigidly imposed from above but rather established by the group itself. As Gelbart remembers:

> To his writers, he was our heavyweight champ. He could and would do anything we asked of him. Our frames of reference became his. There was nothing he didn't understand, providing we understood it. Everything, every subject, was fair game. Nothing was too hip for the room. He had total control, but we had total freedom.[54]

Larry Gelbart pictured the writers as: '. . . a bunch of baby wolves, fighting to win the favor of Sid, the Papa Wolf.' As Caesar remembers it:

> And fight they did. Chunks of plaster were knocked out of the walls; the draperies were ripped to shreds; Mel Brooks frequently was hanged in effigy by the others. But enormous creativity and fresh humor constantly bubbled in that room.[55]

'We all wanted to be Sid's favorite,' says Neil Simon, whose tenure lasted from 1952 to 1954 and again from 1956 to 1957. 'Sid paid better than anybody else. He

53 Rensin, David, 'Hail Caesar.' **www.aarp.org/mmaturity/nov_dec00/cameo.html**
54 Gelbart, Larry, quoted in a transcript of 'Caesar's Hour Revisited,' op. cit.
55 Caesar, Sid. *Where Have I Been?*, op. cit., p. 5.

treated the writers better than any comedian that I ever worked for.'[56]

Caesar's presence in the group was both intimate and direct, yet he allowed individuality to flourish as well. That meant that he was able to listen to his team and learn from them. Like a great band leader, he was able to back off and let his colleagues pursue their own solo performances. In other words, he hired great people and then he let them be great. As Gelbart related:

> In my first days with Sid, he never said a word to me outside the writing room. And he was always there. (One advantage of his omnipresence was that by the time the show aired, he knew every line perfectly.) I was beginning to wonder if I was cutting it with him. And then, after the first show, at the wrap party, he put his arms around me, bent me back as if he were John Gilbert and I were Greta Garbo, and gave me a kiss on the lips. That gesture was his way of saying, 'I appreciate what you've done.' If I'd written him the compliment, he'd have delivered it flawlessly. Left to his own devices, he turned us into a scene from a silent movie.[57]

The end of the run: breaking up a virtuoso team

Towards the end of the 1953–54 television season, rumors began to appear that the virtuoso team that had built *Your Show of Shows* would be dismembered. According to the news outlets:

> The rumors, picked up and printed by TV columnists, indicated that some NBC officials were wondering why

56　Tobias, op. cit.
57　Gelbart, Larry, quoted in a transcript of 'Caesar's Hour Revisited,' op. cit.

so much talent should be used up in a single series. Why not break us up into three, four, or even five series, which would multiply the profits of the network?[58]

Not only were the director and stars – Max Liebman, Sid Caesar and Imogene Coca, respectively – to get their own shows, but the writing team behind it was broken up as well. As Larry Gelbart puts it: 'It was the orig-inal program's success that caused the show to be dismantled, with NBC hoping to get three hits instead of just one by giving Caesar, his co-star, comedienne Imogene Coca, and Liebman each a different show to grind out for the network.'[59] Howard Morris saw it like a product extension decision: 'TV,' he said, 'is like betting on the horses today, and like they say at the racetrack, three winning conversations are better than one.'[60]

At the time, Caesar said:

> The truth of it is that Max, Coca, and myself have to split up because there just isn't time for the three of us to express ourselves on one show any longer. In other words, we've grown-up, and if we hope to continue growing, we must get out on our own. During the past five years, we've done everything that's possible to do within the confines of one show. It's time we're given a chance to express ourselves differently. I know Coca is capable of doing more, and so is Max. There's been a lot of talk around about Max, Coca, and myself breaking up because of friction. That's not true. Your Show of Shows has been a happy road for all of us.[61]

58 Caesar, Sid. *Where Have I Been?*, op. cit., p. 138.
59 Gelbart, Larry, quoted in a transcript of 'Caesar's Hour Revisited,' op. cit.
60 Morris, Howard, quoted in Caesar, Sid. *Where Have I Been?*, op. cit., p. 138.
61 Caesar, Sid. quoted by Marie Torre in *The New York Telegraph*, in Sennett, op. cit., p. 172.

Caesar's new show was to be called *Caesar's Hour*, for which he took part of the core writing team with him. Not surprisingly, of the three shows that emerged from *Your Show of Shows*, only one, *Caesar's Hour*, enjoyed the success of previous efforts. The other two flopped and were quickly canceled. In part, Caesar's continued success was due to his effort to recreate the 'writers' room' for his new show. He says:

The writers' room was crazier than it had been on Your Show of Shows . . .

> Working with such a roomful of geniuses day after day was the most exhilarating time of my life. I was the sole boss. Mine always was the final word on every line and bit of business that went into the show. I even lost my fear of not having Max Liebman around to back me up and edit me. As time went on, that became a problem. As I have since learned, everybody needs an editor . . . [62]

One of the things that Caesar did was to lure Larry Gelbart away from Bob Hope. When Hope learned of Caesar's interest in Gelbart, he wired Caesar: 'Will trade you Larry Gelbart for two oil wells.' But, eventually, Gelbart joined Caesar of his own free will, citing as a reason: 'I liked the idea that you were willing to try any suggestion, no matter how crazy and original it was.'[63]

Ultimately, *Caesar's Hour* fell victim to a variety of forces that led to its demise. Nine years of sustained success is difficult in any entertainment medium, and television is notorious for the capriciousness of its audiences, and new

62 Caesar, Sid. *Where Have I Been?*, op. cit., pp. 145–46.
63 Ibid., p. 144.

technologies such as videotaping took much of the spontaneity out of the craft.

But, for a brief while, there was a team of extraordinary talent that was offered the opportunity to change the world and took full advantage of this chance, repeatedly, over a nine-year period. At the core of this success was a management philosophy that entailed giving talent full independence without sacrificing complete control.

Implications for leading virtuoso teams: Summary and Key Questions

To be one of Sid Caesar's writers was to be at the very pinnacle of your profession. Here was a team that so delighted 'paying' audiences that their sponsor could no longer afford to keep them. Forty years later, this same team had become so influential in the development of their craft that a videotape of their 40th reunion was created and avidly watched by fans and colleagues alike. What did it take to achieve such success?

'Freedom' is at the core of everything that Caesar's writers accomplished. They flourished in an environment where every idea was greeted with the hope that it would be the best idea, ever, and then was immediately improved without the orig-inator feeling in the least bit slighted. What to some might appear chaos was, in fact, a workspace that allowed fast and furious conversation, and at the same time allowed the team leader – Sid Caesar – to be in the very middle of everything going on around him. It's vital to understand that careful attention to managing space and time played a key role for Caesar's team. Space pushed the team together so that direct dialog and intense conversations were impossible to avoid. We can't imagine Caesar's team working with everyone seperated in comfortable cubicles and only coming together for several hours a day. Added to the close physical space were the tight time pressures that helped force direct dialog and the marketplace for ideas. In our experience, space and time are two variables managers too often ignore in their impact on teams and their effectiveness.

This was a team with incredible loyalty to the leader, not because these individual all-stars were predisposed to respect authority – quite the contrary – but because Sid Caesar paid them the ultimate professional compliment: he listened to them; he believed in them; and he trusted them; over and over again.

It was a team of big risk-makers. They rejected the traditional stereotypes of the customer and gave them more, not less. They stretched their audiences with material that was deemed too sophisticated, too thoughtful, and their audience loved it. Key outsiders provided the political cover necessary for the team to take some big risks, and these same outsiders contributed to the team's vision that helped fuel their energy. All in all, this was a great illustration of what is possible when you turn talented people loose to pursue greatness.

From these lessons, there arise a few questions that you should answer when launching your next virtuoso team:

1   Is your virtuoso team truly stretching the customer with their product or experience? Do they think about the customer in ways that are ennobling, and then strive to meet those expectations, or are their views of the customer diminishing ones?

2   Are they stretching themselves? Is their work process pushing them to really engage in a pursuit of outcomes that are well beyond the norm? Is the line between cooperation and competition close enough so that there is real creative license and tension within the group?

3   Are you, or the team leader, personally and centrally engaged in the team's performance? Is this a real hands-on, intimate managerial role for the leader?

4   Are you managing time and space in such a way that the good ideas seem to flow from the group? Is there occasionally a frenetic quality about the cadence of work and a manic passion that characterizes the team? And, is there a willingness to

challenge those ideas, quickly, so as to identify which are worthy of further investment?

5 Is someone providing protective 'cover' for this group, so that the all too familiar bureaucratic dangers are mitigated or reduced?

Lead talent with trust

Miles Davis creates serial innovation through listening and improvisation

> *I never thought that the music called 'jazz' was ever meant to reach just a small group of people, or become a museum thing locked under glass like all the other dead things that were once considered artistic.*[1]
> Miles Davis

On 52nd street in 1950s Manhattan, music was everywhere, and jazz clubs like Minton's and Birdland hosted the very best in contemporary jazz. It was an energetic, competitive, and creative atmosphere, where booze and drugs flowed freely and some of the most exciting music of the century was being created in a setting where ideas and talent moved easily and fast. What relevance could this scene possibly hold for the 21st century manager? A lot, for at the very epicenter of this world was Miles Davis, a jazz trumpeter often described as 'The Prince of Darkness', a most unlikely teacher, yet someone whose story – of a restless innovator striving for and achieving great change – is one that all aspiring leaders should study. Miles Davis revolutionized music at least *three times* over thirty years. This was not luck. Davis continually redefined the popular music of

1 Davis, Miles quoted on **www.photomatt.net/jazzquotes**.

his time, each time working with a different 'all-star' team that he had personally assembled and led. How did he accomplish this? How did he assemble and inspire his teams of all-stars to achieve great things? What can we learn from the experience – the chemistry – of these groups and the way that Miles Davis exercised leadership talent?

In this chapter, we'll learn how Miles Davis accomplished these achievements with three different virtuoso teams. Insights for today's managers should readily emerge. We'll see how he was preoccupied by getting the best talent obtainable and how he then took this talent and made the most of it. We'll learn that Miles, like many virtuoso leaders, was a minimalist when it came to direction. His style was to truly trust the superb assembled talent to exercise their full genius and to utilize their personal skills and professional knowledge in their own way to achieve the objectives that he had established. We'll learn that this is not necessarily an easy or 'natural' way to manage. We'll see teams looking for more rather than less direction from the top, because they were unaccustomed to being trusted; virtuosos who were nonplussed by having more freedom than they had ever experienced. We'll also see why being a member of a Miles Davis band was both an incredible learning experience and an incredibly stressful experience. We'll see a team environment where expectations were high, and feedback immediate and direct. Where the leader was continually central and engaged, and where the next generation of professional leadership was always being developed.

Davis, one of the greatest trumpeters of all time, was a catalyst for high performance in an all-star team context. Never content, constantly restless, forever looking for change, he always wanted to the push the limits. The great bass player Ron Carter may have said it best when he recognized that Miles Davis: '. . . was one of the few who was able to turn the world of music in any direction he chose.'[2] What is remarkable about Davis and this story is that he *did* choose to change the world of music, and he did it three times. In this regard, we'll see a leader who was constantly experimenting with team membership and how to configure the available talent. He was essentially building 'prototypes,' an important concept found in virtuoso teams throughout this book. Only, in this case Davis was altering the team, in an effort to improve their output.

Finally, we'll meet a leader who was a great listener. We believe that 'listening' to each team member is a critical competency for a leader of virtuosos. Like other great virtuoso team leaders, Davis understood that the team knew more than he did and he led appropriately. Given the definition of virtuosity, and the notion that in these teams you have a true expert at each position, listening is essential. It is hard to believe that a leader in such situations can think they know more than their team members. Sadly, they often don't listen, they tell. In such cases, as Miles Davis will illustrate, listening is a good way for the leader to spend their time.

Miles Davis: a driven innovator who became a catalytic leader

Miles Davis was a consummate knowledge professional. Raised in jazz through boyhood trumpet lessons, he was also briefly exposed to the wider world of classical music at the Julliard Academy in New York. The composer David Amram suggests that Davis constantly changed styles and interests, 'because he had such broad interest in so many things and was so perceptive.'[3] Another observer has noted that Davis had an acute fascination with differences: 'One

2 Carter, Ron, quoted in '"Any Direction He Chose": Ron Carter interview by Benjamin Cawthra,' in Early, Gerald (ed.). *Miles Davis and American Culture*. St. Louis: Missouri Historical Society Press, 2001.

of Miles's great strengths became his capacity for transforming differences into unifying bridges, a characteristic that was epitomized by his music, his work with musicians of a wide variety of musical, ethnic, racial, and cultural origins, and his appeal to audiences of equally varied backgrounds.'[4] Like many a great leader/manager, he was never content with the status quo.

Davis was also a very capable leader: he demanded change and made it happen. Pianist Ahmad Jamal believes that Miles Davis' groups were successful, in part, because he was a tough leader:

> Everything depends upon the leader. You can have great musicians. But if your whole demeanor, your whole image is weak, you're going to have a weak group. So you have to be strong. You must be almost tyrannical. And Miles was a strong personality.
>
> He had many great groups . . . He didn't ever have a weak group . . . He had that uncanny knack of selecting those people that complimented him to the utmost. But here again, the reason why those groups were successful was because of Miles.[5]

The first all-star team: combining brilliant talent with great ideas

In 1949, after establishing his own credentials and reputation as a leading young musician, Davis assembled

3 Amram, David, quoted in Szwed, John. *So What: The Life of Miles Davis.* New York: Simon & Schuster, 2002, p. 131.
4 Tingen, Paul. *Miles Beyond.* New York: BillBoard Books, 2001, p. 29.
5 Jamal, Ahmad, quoted in "Sensational Pulse,' Ahmad Jamal, interview by Benjamin Cawthra,' in Early, Gerald (ed.), *Miles Davis and American Culture.* St. Louis: Missouri Historical Society Press, 2001.

an all-star group – his nonet – made-up of nine great young musicians who were looking for a chance to display their talent. They were all hand-picked and they were all extremely talented. Just being asked to play on the team was recognition of success. Trombonist Mike Zwerin expressed it best when he said: '[i]t was fun being on a championship team.'[6] The team included such great individual performers as: Davis on trumpet; Kai Winding and J.J. Johnson on trombone; Lee Konitz on alto saxophone; Gerry Mulligan on baritone saxophone; Al Haig and John Lewis on piano; Kenny Clarke and Max Roach on drums; Gunther Schuller on French horn; and Gil Evans as senior arranger. This group represents a 'hall of fame' for jazz enthusiasts. The music that they created, the *Birth of the Cool*, moved jazz away from the then prevailing sound of bop towards the whole new sound of 'cool.'

Besides being great musicians, they were also smart guys; a group of true professionals who understood their art and, beyond that, were devoted to 'ideas.' They gathered nightly at a small apartment owned by arranger Gil Evans, which sat next to a Chinese laundry, and they spoke endlessly about old and new types of music – classical and jazz, bop and what was missing in bop. People came and went, the door was always open. They sat on the bed; they sat on the floor; it was chaotic. It was an unceasing, freewheeling, challenging and energizing conversation that centered the members on the power of ideas and what it would take to launch a musical revolution and overthrow the current dominance of bebop.

6 Zwerin, Mike. Liner notes for *Complete Birth of the Cool*. Capital Jazz, 1998.

As important as the resulting music, however, was the pattern that begins with this group, which was for Miles Davis to surround himself throughout his career with the very best talent. Nat Hentoff, the great jazz writer, saw this in Davis when he wrote: 'The essence of Miles Davis can be determined by listening to the men he has surrounded himself with on his regular jobs.' Hentoff quotes Davis as saying of drummer Philly Joe Jones, for instance, 'I wouldn't care if he came up on the bandstand in his BVD's and with one arm, just so long as he was there. He's got the fire I want. There's nothing more terrible than playing with a dull rhythm section. Jazz has got to have that thing.'[7]

The emergence of a distinctive leadership philosophy

The *Birth of the Cool* nonet was Davis' first leadership role and it was not immediately apparent that he was good at it. During 1948, while they struggled to establish the group, the members were dispersed among the various bands that they were currently playing for in order to continue to earn a living. Yet despite this concession to reality, the nonet nonetheless considered themselves a team, and there were real concerns about the leadership of Miles within the fledgling group:

> John Lewis got really upset with Miles . . . [when he felt that] Miles refused to assume control. He thought if you got problems, they'll solve themselves. You know, things don't work themselves out in bands. Somebody has to make it come together, and I suppose that being Miles' first band, he hadn't come to grips with that, so the first

7 Goldbeg, Joe. *Jazz Masters of the 50s*. New York: DeCapo Press, 1965, p. 75.

band, when it went out to play in clubs . . . [it] began running into a whole new set of problems. About phrasing, and playing together, and so on . . . somebody has to lay down the rules . . . if there's a choice, somebody has to make the choice.

John Lewis would keep trying to tell him, 'Miles, you went out and got the gig for this. This is not a rehearsal band any more. If you want to be the leader, then you've got to be the leader.' Miles would say, 'Bullshit, man. Problems have got to take care of themselves.'[8]

These early challenges to his leadership style are related to the core of the philosophy Davis had about leading talented knowledge professionals. What was thought to be Miles' uncertainty and his lack of willingness to 'take charge', was more likely the result of his seeing the nonet as a collaborative team, rather than seeing himself as the center of the band. He believed that all of the team members were experts in their own right. Leading from the center would only diminish the skills and motivations of those on the team. Therefore, in the spirit of full collaboration, Davis surprised the arrangers of the music – Gerry Mulligan, Gil Evans and John Lewis – by sharing the billing at the group's public opening. It was an unprecedented gesture, but one that made a powerful statement about how he regarded the contribution of the talent he had assembled.[9]

While the nonet's talent was indisputable, selecting it was not without risk. In particular, Davis was strongly

8 Interviews for *The Miles Davis Radio Project*, 1990, produced by Steve Roland, as quoted in Szwed, op. cit., pp. 74–75.
9 Chambers, Jack. *Milestones: The Music and Times of Miles Davis*. New York: De Capo, 1998, pp. 102–103.

criticized within the African-American community for picking so many white players. Davis, who was identified throughout his career for his racial pride, repeatedly put talent before skin color in assembling his groups:

> So I just told them that if a guy could play as good as Lee Konitz played – that's who they were mad about most, because there were a lot of black alto players around – I would hire him every time, and I wouldn't give a damn if he was green with red breath.[10]

This was a risky undertaking. The music was different and made new requirements on both players and listeners. Count Basie, whose band was appearing along with the nonet, put it more succinctly, but still admiringly: 'I didn't always know what they (the nonet) were doing, but I listened, and I liked it.'[11]

The nonet was, without argument, an all-star team, but one that like so many virtuoso teams was not destined to last long. Opportunities flew at the members and they pursued their brilliant careers independently. For a handful of precious weeks, the nonet had brought together extraordinary talent, planting the seeds for future revolutions in jazz. The nonet was also a 'crucible' for leadership growth for Davis. He experienced leadership challenges that he was unprepared for. The simple act of getting nine great virtuoso musicians together, and then to produce a revolutionary body of work, turned out to be anything but 'simple.' What the nonet experience did, however, was to school Davis in such critical leadership

10 Davis, Miles. *Miles, the Autobiography.* Quoted in Szwed, op. cit., p. 76.
11 Chambers, Jack. *Milestones: The Music and Times of Miles Davis.* New York: De Capo, 1998, p. 106.

issues as: risk-making, talent identification, leadership behavior and its effect on motivation and creativity, and assumptions of market receptivity towards radical innovation.

The second all-star team: prototyping talent configurations

By 1956 Miles Davis had assembled a new team. This time a quintet, including saxophonist John Coltrane, pianist Red Garland, drummer Philly Joe Jones, and bassist Paul Chambers, that was one of the greatest jazz bands in history. It also illustrates how Davis as leader molded a team and dealt with strong egos and extraordinary talent. Jazz writer Ralph Gleason described the way the band worked as:

> The intricacy of the linkage between the minds of these musicians has never been equaled in any group, in my opinion.[12]

The output of this group was six albums that moved away from 'cool' and established what was called 'hard bop.' Was this a fourth revolution? It's hard to say, but the music was great, and the musicians extraordinary. Despite the success of this group, however, Davis once again was restless. He was not satisfied with where the music was taking him, nor where he was taking the music.

In 1957, Davis joined Columbia Records, which was not only the leading popular music label of its time, but

---

12 Kahn, Ashley. *Kind of Blue: The Making of the Miles Davis Masterpiece.* New York: De Capo Press, 2001, p. 57.

which also had an experimental, innovative culture. Columbia was known to take risks and to support imaginative and thoughful experimentation in music. It was the perfect sponsor for another revolution, and Davis had an idea for a new vision of jazz. In 1958, he was thinking about music that would, '. . . be freer, more modal, more African or Eastern and less Western.'[13] Once again collaborating with arranger Gil Evans, the result was an entirely new type of music, called 'modal.'

By late May 1958, Davis had assembled the sextet that would create 'modal' music. They would work together for seven months, culminating in the recording of *Kind of Blue*. The group's roots were the great quintet of a few years earlier, but with some interesting personnel changes. It consisted of, besides Miles Davis on trumpet: John Coltrane (tenor sax), Cannonball Adderley (alto sax), Wynton Kelly or Bill Evans (piano), Jimmy Cobb (drums) and Paul Chambers (bass).

It was an unusual band in that it had two saxophonists – great ones – which was certainly a departure from the norm, for both the music and the players. The effect of two saxophones was significant: 'The musical effect was like turning the heat up on a pressure cooker: Coltrane would have less time to solo onstage, and there was an additional voice (and a very fluid, assertive one at that) to interact with, play off of, and factor into the band's total sound.'[14] Despite this experiment, the band did not take long to gel. The speed with which the team fell together surprised even Davis: 'Faster than I could have imagined,

13 Kahn, Ibid., pp. 98–9.
14 Kahn, Ibid., p. 66.

the music that we were playing together was just unbelievable. It was so bad that it used to send chills through me at night.'[15] [In this instance 'bad' is an admirable term: this music was great.]

As with all of his groups, the talent was dazzling. Davis had a growing reputation for identifying young talent and attracting it like a magnet. In 1957, he was in competition with legendary trumpeter Dizzy Gillespie for the services of saxaphonist Cannonball Adderley. Adderley joined Davis. In his words: 'I figured I could learn more than with Dizzy. Not that Dizzy isn't a good teacher, but he played more commercially than Miles. Thank goodness I made the move I did.'[16] Davis also recognized John Coltrane's talent well before others did. Despite earlier disciplinary problems with Coltrane, his return to Miles Davis' band really launched Coltrane's future superstar career. Davis provided, 'Coltrane [with] creative license rather than explicit direction – the tenor saxophonist was cajoled and challenged into an individual direction that sired an entirely new school of jazz.'[17] Bill Evans later described the unswayable faith that Miles had in his new team member:

> I don't think we would've had Coltrane's great contributions without Miles' belief in his potential. Because at the beginning, most people wondered why Miles had Coltrane in the group – he was more or less a withdrawn presence on the bandstand, not fumbling exactly, but just sort of searching. But Miles really knew, somehow, the development that Coltrane had coming.[18]

15 Kahn, Ibid., p. 50.
16 Kahn, Ibid., p. 64.
17 Kahn, Ibid., p. 49.
18 Kahn, Ibid., p. 49.

Evans himself was also a controversial choice for several of the band members, who had wanted a more assertive sound than he brought, and he was white, but Davis insisted that he had to have him. When the group was playing in black clubs, 'and guys would come up to us and say: "What's that white guy doing here?" They said: "Miles wants him there – he's supposed to be there!"'[19] Davis, in fact, later wrote that he: 'had already planned that album [*Kind of Blue*] around the piano playing of Bill Evans.'

Prototyping virtuoso talent configurations

Having attracted all-star talent to his team, Davis as a leader was not afraid to challenge this talent with surprises and twists and turns in their expected roles, in an effort to push them to a higher level of performance. In the making of the *Birth of the Cool* recording Davis, intentionally or otherwise, had not bothered to apprise his current pianist, Wynton Kelly, of his decision to use (not to mention building the music around) Bill Evans as his pianist. This came as a complete surprise to Kelly, who showed up for the recording session fully expecting to be at the piano, only to find Evans there instead. According to drummer Jimmy Cobb:

> When Wynton arrived at the studio to record Kind of Blue he saw Bill sitting at the piano and was flabbergasted! He said, 'Damn, I rushed all the way over here and someone else is sitting at the piano!'[20]

The first track recorded was 'Freddie Freeloader,' which had Kelly on piano. Perhaps this was recorded first to

19 Kahn, Ibid., pp. 83–5.
20 Kahn, Ibid., p. 95.

soothe Kelly's ruffled feathers and minimize the amount of time that he had to wait around the session? At any rate, after that, it was Bill Evans on the piano for all of the further tracks, and some observers contend that the one track that Kelly was in was one of his finest performances ever. By deliberately putting Evans and Kelly into a direct and uncomfortable competitive situation, Davis was able to get extraordinary performances out of both pianists.

Miles Davis also prototyped other combinations of talent in ways never tried before. His experiments with the two pianists and the two saxophonists were not random. Nat Adderley, Cannonball's brother and a fine trumpet player in his own right, said that: 'Miles rubbed one player against the other to get what he wanted from his music.' Challenging the team to establish new emotional and intellectual intimacy was a way Davis ensured growth, development, and innovation:

> Miles would go say to Cannonball, 'You ought to listen to what Coltrane is doing and the way he's got a whole philosophy of sound going.' Then he goes and tells Trane [John Coltrane], 'You should listen to Cannonball. He gets himself across with more utilitarian use of notes.'[21]

Davis' insistence on the 'best talent obtainable,' rather than merely the 'best available' can also be seen in his actions on another Gil Evans collaboration, *Sketches of Spain*, where Davis insisted on having lead trombonist Frank Rehak as one of the team:

> When Rehak told Gil [Evans] that he wasn't available for Sketches of Spain, he received a call at 3:30 a.m.: 'Hey, mother, what are doing to me?' It was Miles . . . and I

21 Adderley, Nat quoted in Szwed, op. cit., p. 172.

said, 'Man, there's no way I can do those dates.' And he said, 'Listen, I'll give you double money, I'll give you whatever you need.' Rehak explained that it was not a question of money. He was already booked for a number of sessions, and canceling would be bad for his career. 'We haggled and haggled for about fifteen minutes, and he called me several different kinds of names, and there was nothing I could do.' He was available only three hours on one day, three on another, and a few hours on a third. At seven the next morning, [producer] Ted Macero called Rehak, wanting to know what he had on Miles, since he was refusing to do the record without him. In the end, nineteen musicians and several engineers all had their schedules changed to fit Rehak's on the date.[22]

Leading through trust within the team

Davis' groups were also well known for the directness of their conversations. There was no time wasted on unnecessary politeness. The sparseness of conversation focused almost entirely on achieving better performance, and no one was spared. On the tracks of *Kind of Blue*, the following dialog can be heard:

> In recording 'Blue in Green,' Miles Davis: 'Use both hands, Jimmy.' Jimmy Cobb: 'Huh?' Miles Davis: 'Just use both hands and play it the best way you can, you know. It'll be alright.'[23]

> At the end of a take for 'Blue in Green,' Miles 'rides' Chambers for his handling of the ending . . . Miles Davis: 'Wake up, Paul.'[24]

22 Szwed, op. cit., p. 211.
23 Kahn, op. cit., p. 119.
24 Kahn, op. cit., p. 121.

> During the second recording session, on one of the takes
> for *Sketches*, MD to Paul Chambers: 'You're not watching
> Bill [Evans].' Paul Chambers: 'I know. I'm sorry.'[25]

Throughout his career, Miles Davis demonstrated
enormous trust in the capabilities of the people he had
assembled and constantly looked for ways of providing
maximum creative space for them. This was as true for the
Kind of Blue sextet as it was for all of his other groups.

'If Miles prepared any written directions for *Kind of Blue*,
they would have been a few motifs sketched on staff
paper.' ('It could have been done on a napkin, the forms
were so simple,' notes bandleader and reissue producer
Bob Belden.) Davis later admitted: 'I didn't write out the
music for *Kind of Blue*, but brought in sketches for what
everybody was supposed to play because I wanted a lot of
spontaneity in the playing.'[26] Drummer Jimmy Cobb
recalls: 'Mostly he would just say: "This is straight time"
or "This is three," "Latin flavored" or "This is whatever
you want."' Bill Evans recalled: 'Miles ran over the charts
a couple of times. You know, 'Do this,' 'Do that' and then
he laid out a structure, like: 'You solo first.' Sometimes
during a take we didn't even know that . . . Once we had
the chart straight, the rest was up for grabs.'[27]

This reliance on talent to make the right calls was
something that Miles Davis used most effectively in getting
full value from the talent that he had assembled, and was
illustrated most emphatically in his relationship with the
great saxophonist John Coltrane. According to Davis:

25 Kahn, op. cit., p. 140.
26 Kahn, op. cit., p. 99.
27 Kahn, op. cit., p. 99.

> I think the reason we didn't get along at first was because Trane liked to ask all these motherf***ing questions back then about what he should or shouldn't play. Man, f*** that shit; to me he was a professional musician, and I have always wanted whoever played with me to find their own place in the music. So my silence and evil looks probably turned him off.[28]

As Cannonball Adderley recalled in 1972: 'When [Miles] did speak, it was typically to react to something that seemed out of place. He never told anyone what to play but would say: 'Man, you don't need to do that.' Miles really told everybody what NOT to do. I heard him and dug it.'[29]

The result was great talent playing to its maximum potential. Saxophonist Wayne Shorter, who later was part of Davis' great fusion group, spoke about first hearing a Miles Davis band:

> I went into the audience and sat and waited until the band came on . . . I was listening to the power of individualism and subjectivity that was going on with all the players. Cannonball, Coltrane, and whoever was playing piano at the time, probably Wynton Kelly, and Paul Chambers on bass. They opened with a song called 'All Blues' and what I heard and felt was penetrating. The music seemed to transport the audience to some place they don't usually go in their everyday life.[30]

As one observer put it: 'A home run every time one of them soloed.'[31] The extent to which this band represented a real revolution in jazz can be vividly found in a conversation between the vocalist Shirley Horn, and the

28 Kahn, op. cit., p. 50.
29 Kahn, op. cit., p. 106.
30 Shorter, Wayne, quoted in Szwed, op. cit., p. 252.
31 Costello, Del, quoted in Kahn, op. cit., p. 156.

great jazz saxaphonist Stan Getz, shortly after the
appearance of *Kind of Blue*:

> I remember we were playing in New York at some hotel
> bar and I was on break and I went . . . up to Stan Getz,
> who was there. We hugged and then we stood there and
> listened [to Kind of Blue]. I said, 'What do you think?' He
> said, 'I don't know what to think . . . ' I said, 'I don't
> either.' It was beautiful but confusing.[32]

Bill Evans believed that 'it was the greatest jazz band [he]
had ever heard.'[33]

After July 1959, at the height of its success, the band
disassembled. Evans, Coltrane, Adderley and Kelly were
ready to lead their own groups. All of them had great
careers; Evans and Coltrane themselves changed the
future face of jazz. According to Jimmy Cobb:

> The *Kind of Blue* thing did separate into a variety of all-
> star groups because the band was an all-star kind of band
> in the first place, and most of it was different flavors.[34]

The third all-star group: building a legendary team from great individuals using controlled freedom

By May 1963, Davis was once again restless for change
and challenge. Once again, he assembled a new quintet,
this time including 26-year-old bassist Ron Carter, 23-
year-old pianist Herbie Hancock, and 17-year-old
drummer Tony Williams, along with saxophonist Wayne

32 Horn, Shirley, quoted in Kahn, op. cit., p. 160.
33 Kahn, op. cit., p. 86.
34 Cobb, Jimmy, quoted in Kahn, op. cit., p. 161.

Shorter, all of whom were destined for future superstardom in the jazz world. This band came to be generally known as 'the second great quintet' – in deference to the 'first great quintet' which consisted of Coltrane, Red Garland (piano), Chambers and Philly Joe Jones (drums), and was described by Amiri Baraka (LeRoi Jones) as the 'all-time classical hydrogen bomb and switchblade band.'[35]

Once again this was a team committed to revolution and, as always when revolution is the goal, there is often a fine line between brilliance and excess. Davis often walked this line – he was always taking risks, trying things, prototyping, and yet he needed to satisfy the market's expectations as well. Herbie Hancock put it this way:

> [We wanted our audience to be] . . . hearing the avant-garde on the one hand, and . . . hearing the history of jazz that led up to it on the other hand – because Miles was that history. He was that link. We were sort of walking a tightrope with the kind of experimenting we were doing in music, not total experimentation, but we used to call it 'controlled freedom.'[36]

Hancock recalls that they wanted to play 'against expectations,' and Shorter speaks of 'taking chances' and of 'struggling with music.'[37]

From one set to the next over two nights at the Plugged Nickel, they were changing these tunes, shifting their tempos around, and stretching their forms to the breaking point. At times, it became messy and chaotic, but

---

35 Baraka, Amiri, quoted in Szwed, op. cit., p. 252.
36 Hancock, Herbie, quoted in Szwed, op. cit., p. 255.
37 Szwed, op. cit., p. 255.

thrillingly so. Yet it was all accomplished with a mutuality, confidence, and openness to chance that is rare in music and life.[38] Not all teams can do this, and bassist Ron Carter speculated on why he was hired by Davis, along with Herbie Hancock and Tony Williams:

> My general sense of it is that he picked three guys who he thought could help him make some 'new' music. He seemed to have the ability to always put together the kind of groups that would make it easier to do the kind of music he was looking to do, whether it was Paul [Chambers], Wynton [Kelly], and Jimmy Cobb, or Paul [Chambers], Bill Evans, and Jimmy Cobb, or Philly [Joe Jones], and Paul [Chambers], and Red [Garland]. He seemed to find the combination of rhythm section players to make whatever he was looking for more easily found. In those five years none of us looked at him as a guy who put together these three people for his music. We just knew he'd hired us. And I think not until many years later would we have sat down and said, 'Wow, this is the reason why we were chosen.'[39]

It was Wayne Shorter's opinion that: 'Miles wanted to play with people who knew more about music than he did . . . He wasn't afraid of it.'[40]

This group, unlike previous ones that Davis had worked with, and unlike the tradition of jazz groups in general, composed most of the music it played, and they were composing 'groundbreaking' work at that.[41] In addition,

38 Szwed, op. cit., pp. 255–56.
39 Carter, Ron, quoted in "Any Direction He Chose,': Ron Carter interview byBenjamin Cawthra,' in Early, Gerald (ed.). *Miles Davis and American Culture*. St. Louis: Missouri Historical Society Press, 2001.
40 Shorter, Wayne, quoted in Szwed, op. cit., p. 256.
41 Tingen, op. cit., p. 36.

and perhaps because of their multi-talented backgrounds, Davis arranged this group in a way that made the rhythm section equal with the front line. Again, this was a departure from the norm, and one which gave greater recognition to all of the members who were involved in making this new music. Once again, we see Davis innovating as a leader in order to create more rather than fewer opportunities for his assembled talent to achieve their individual promise. An interview with pianist Ahmad Jamal reveals what Davis was looking for in and from his team:

> I think he saw [his team] as individuals . . . I think he sought those people for what they were worth within themselves.[42]

And then he created a context, which allowed them to get there. It was the power of the individual, within a group context, that marks the genius of Miles Davis. This was not typical of the jazz world, yet it was the leitmotif which ran through Davis' career, from the movement from bop to cool, to the group that created *Kind of Blue*, to his later fusion bands.

For most jazz groups, the improvised solo is the ultimate goal, the highest level of achievement. The composition on which they improvise and the accompaniment that frames the solos are both secondary. Typically, the leader is the best improviser, or at least the featured soloist, and the rest of the group exists to enhance the soloist's

42 Jamal, Ahmad, quoted in "Sensational Pulse,' Ahmad Jamal, interview byBenjamin Cawthra,' in Early, Gerald (ed.). *Miles Davis and American Culture*. St. Louis: Missouri Historical Society Press, 2001.

mastery. What was different about the Davis group [here the author, John Szwed, is talking about the Hancock-Williams-Carter band, but it could apply to any of Davis' great groups] was his attitude toward the individual musicians and how they should work together. Tony Williams said that Davis hired people who were good, but he encouraged them to be better, to take chances, even to go beyond him if they chose. 'He wants to hear stuff he's not in control of,' Tony said. 'He wants to hear something that he wouldn't think of. I mean, when he walks off the stage, he's not just going to go and, you know, read a book or something. He wants to hear the music still going on at a level that he left it at or something better.'[43]

To Miles Davis, the challenge was to build a group out of superbly-gifted individuals, where the team was much more than merely the sum of the individuals [or what all too often in team situations is *less* than the sum of the individuals] – in terms of creativity, innovation and performance:

> We realized that Miles was looking for [a] collective improvisation thing with all these different people who had different styles. Miles was looking for unity in the collective.[44]

Recognition of the power of a team was also evidenced in Davis' respect for what they had accomplished together. He was once asked if the time in which he did *Bitches Brew* was one of his most creative periods. 'It was *their* creative period,' was his response – Joe Zawinul's, his musicians'. All he did, he said, was to make it possible for them to play together.[45]

43 Szwed, op. cit., p. 263.
44 DeJohnette, Jack, quoted in Szwed, John. *So What* op. cit., p. 295.
45 Szwed, op. cit., p. 299.

Despite this belief in individual freedom the leadership position was, nonetheless, a strong and respected role. Chick Corea recognized that: 'Miles was brilliant as a bandleader. He allowed the musicians to play just as they are and deal with the music from their own choices and their own judgments. Therefore the music that came out was very strong.'[46] Bassist Michael Henderson put it even more strongly:

> Miles gave me myself. He gave me something that belonged to me. When I came to play with him, I became 'me.' Like everybody else who was with him. We all found ourselves. We found exactly who we were and what we should be doing as far as being in the music industry, and in life.[47]

One of the ways that Miles Davis tried to get the most out of this quintet was to encourage them to think about things they could do that they didn't know they could do. His instructions were frequently given in ways that encouraged individual interpretation, such as telling them: 'Don't play what's there. Play what's not there.'[48] Occasionally, they were about desired outcomes, not how to do the work. For example, Wayne Shorter relates that: 'Miles once said, 'Did you ever go to see that movie where Humphrey Bogart is talking to a gangster and does that bam-ba-bam-bam?' He mimes Bogart, in *The Maltese Falcon*, knocking a cigarette out of Peter Lorre's mouth. 'Play that!' or the way John Wayne walks in *The Searchers*.'[49]

---

46 Corea, Chick quoted in Tingen, op. cit. p. 48.
47 Tingen, op. cit., p. 17.
48 Tingen, op. cit., p. 14.
49 Honigmann, David. 'Shorter Route to Jazz Heaven,' *Financial Times*, March 8, 2003.

Despite his well-earned reputation for direct dialog, there was also total trust in the capabilities of his team. As bassist Dave Holland saw it:

> I got the sense that if he felt he had to explain to someone too much then he had the wrong musician for the project.[50]

Leadership in such a group was very much about insisting on change, on being a catalyst for change. In this last group, Davis relied a lot on 'guest' membership in the team to introduce new ideas. In 1970, Miles hired Motown bassist Michael Henderson. According to Henderson:

> He hired me to play just what I was playing. He hired me to bring something new to his music. I thought that maybe he wanted me to learn some of his older stuff, but he said, 'If you learn any of that old shit, you're fired!' [51]

For Miles Davis, music and what he did was all about new ideas: 'I'm happy if I can play one new idea on a night,' and he mentioned in his autobiography that he: 'learned something new every night and the songs [they] played at the beginning of the year were often unrecognizable by the end of the year.'[52]

What we also see in this period is a measure of Davis' own personal maturity as a mover and changer in the music world. Paul Tingen, the chronicler of his 'electronic period' notes: 'Miles was continuously in the center of attention. His commanding here-and-now presence forced the musicians, once again, to 'play above what they

50 Szwed, op. cit., p. 293.
51 Tingen, op. cit., p. 119.
52 Tingen, op. cit., p. 24.

normally play."[53] Such 'stretching' of his talent involved personal risks, for all involved. Drummer Jack DeJohnette reflected on this:

> People were often worried about their personal contributions and egos, but Miles was thinking of it as a team.[54]

Davis, himself, however, was apparently able to subdue his own ego within these groups. In the words of his last partner, Jo Gelbard:

> He had no ego in music . . . As opposed to, 'This is Miles Davis, and who cares who's behind me.' It was never about him and his horn. He was always part of the group that was with him.[55]

Or, as Herbie Hancock expressed it:

> Miles is an incredible team worker. He listens to what everybody does, and he uses that and what he plays makes what everybody does sound better.[56]

There was, in addition, an undeniable love of making music that inspired everyone that was part of his team. The great pianist Chick Corea put it this way:

> Miles set an example by the way he loved to make music. He was about making music. That kind of attitude created an atmosphere in which we all joined, because we all wanted to make music in such a very concentrated way.[57]

---

53 Tingen, op. cit., p. 27.
54 Tingen, op. cit., p. 17.
55 Tingen, op. cit., p. 16
56 Tingen, op. cit., p. 17.
57 Tingen, op. cit., p. 18.

The music that this band created launched a revolution in jazz that changed the nature of the music and the very instruments that we take for granted in such music making. In addition, it launched the careers of an entire generation of new jazz leaders, including Herbie Hancock, Chick Corea and Wayne Shorter.

A few final words about Miles Davis: listener and teacher

Over the years, the reputation of Miles Davis has been stretched out of proportion by media fixations on his personal failings. Colleagues, friends, family, and even his personal brand were all victims of Davis' destructive tendencies. But beneath all of this was an artist who had the courage, the creativity, the resolve, and the humility, to effectively and profoundly change the world of music at least three times. Two characteristics of his personal style bear mentioning. First, Davis was a virtuoso listener. In the words of bassist Gary Peacock: 'He'd listen so hard that it was deafening. He didn't miss anything.'[58] Peacock called Davis: 'by far the greatest listener that I have ever experienced in a musical group.' And, keyboardist Adam Holzman says: 'It may be a funny thing to say for a musician, but Miles taught me how to listen.'[59] In fact, the very first word in Miles Davis' autobiography is 'Listen.' We believe that without his skills as a listener, he could never have been an effective leader. Second, he was also very much a teacher. Joey DeFrancesco was 17 when he played keyboard for Miles Davis in 1988. When asked:

58 Szwed, op. cit., p. 256.
59 All of the quotes in this paragraph come from Tingen, op. cit., p. 14.

'What had he learned from this experience?', his response is quite revealing:

> Oh, all kinds of stuff. I learned to take chances, not try to be so careful. You know, go for it. If you're going for it, you're going to make some mistakes, but that's cool, because the instrument, man, it's your voice. It's an extension of what you're doing. And about harmony, and how to take one note, man, and make it sound like everything everybody else did was nothing. He was the master of that. And I learned how beautiful it was to play ballads and stuff and how great a ballad can be, because when you're younger you don't want to play that stuff. I learned a lot of things.[60]

As saxophonist Sonny Sharrock told radio DJ Ed Flynn in 1993:

> Miles gave me a piece of torn music paper with this impossible to play figure, a 16th note figure, just incredible music, torn-off corner of music, and he said [hoarse whisper], 'Play this'. That's how he did it, you know. And then I would mess up; he would say, 'Naw, Sonny, not like that', you know. But I learned more playing with that cat in one day than I've ever learned in my life, man. He was an incredible teacher, just being around him.[61]

It is not surprising that eventually the Miles Davis experience became known amongst young jazz musicians as 'the University of Miles Davis.'[62] Not a bad epitaph for someone who is so often considered to have been such a troubled and deeply flawed individual.

60 De Francesco, Joey, as quoted in "Here's God Walking Around': Joey DeFrancesco interview by Benjamin Cawthra,' in Early, Gerald (ed.). *Miles Davis and American Culture*. St. Louis: Missouri Historical Society Press, 2001.
61 'The Jack Johnson Sessions,' *The Wire*, October 2003.
62 Tingen, op. cit., p. 26

Implications for leading virtuoso teams: Summary and Key Questions

Creating revolution in any field is extremely rare; to do it three times (or maybe four – *hard bop*) is extraordinary. It is not luck. Miles Davis did it by assembling the best talent obtainable, position by position, and then creating an environment where they could perform at their own individual all-star level, but within a team context. To work in a Miles Davis band was, in and of itself, a badge of achievement. These guys were an elite, they knew it, and were allowed to play like one. We believe that this is an important lesson. Creating teams, position by position, to display virtuoso strength is a key requirement for achieving *big change*. In too many instances, however, we see just the reverse. Great goals are pursued using teams assembled from the talent available, and selected on the basis of how they work together, rather than the potential that they represent.

Having assembled great talent, Davis then pushed it to levels of accomplishment that were beyond even what they thought was attainable. He had no hesitation in rearranging and innovating with team members and configurations in ways that are reminiscent of prototyping. This was always done in an attempt to put people in positions that stretched them out of their comfort zones and challenged them to be even better than they already were. It was not popular, but Davis was focused on results, not feelings. Again, we think that this is important when *big change* is the objective. Too often, contemporary management practice is biased towards building teams whose hallmark is conviviality rather than performance. They are harmonious and work well together but the results are not the principal concern, and *big change* might remain only a dream. We think that this is a blueprint for mediocrity. We believe that talent is too scarce and precious to waste time focusing on being cordial. Cordial is fine, but not if it gets in the way of big ideas and the *big change* needed to make them happen. Contentiousness can often be more effective in bringing to the surface the big ideas that are considered and challenged. Striving for greatness is not comfortable and it isn't always polite. We also think that the conversations that fuel the group's idea work must be direct and instructive. To play in a Miles Davis' band was to be fair game for criticism. Yet at the same time, you were also sure to learn a lot, no matter how good you were to start with. We think that you should be creating team norms that value great ideas more than harmonious work situations. We also think that conflict-avoiding politeness is too often a barrier to fast and effective conversation. Along with the challenge and surprises, Davis' teams were also characterized by trust and respect. Davis was the consummate listener. He knew what was going on within his team, and outside as well, all of the time. He might not know as much as his people, but he knew the right questions to ask.

This is key for managers of virtuoso teams. Not knowing as much as the team members should be taken for granted, but it doesn't absolve the leader of being uninvolved. Davis was anything but that. He was always in the center of the team; in the center of the action; and, of course, he was always listening: for talent, for ideas, for prototyping. The whole idea was about great results and several generations of jazz musicians were schooled in the University of Miles Davis. Finally, we think that you should strive to build a learning legacy of your own, in your teams, in the spirit of that university. What better tribute to an effective leader could there be than to have learning be part of their personal brand?

From these lessons there arise a few questions that you should answer when launching your next virtuoso team:

1 When *big change* is the goal, do you truly insist on doing everything possible to assemble the best talent obtainable, no matter where it is located? Or do you instead use the people available, even when you know that they are not the best possible?

2 Is it possible for your organization to provide sufficient internal mobility so that the best talent can be called upon when needed, even by other departments or functions?

3 Do you strive to preserve individual excellence within a team context? Do you let the 'I's' surface, or overly obsess about the 'we's'?

4 Do you take great individual talent and somehow diminish it to a group average in the way in which you establish team behavioral norms? Or do you let the expertise truly rise and let consensus and democracy fall by the wayside at times?

5 Do you establish the overall parameters that you desire for your people, and then let them get on with figuring out how to achieve these? Or do you not only set the goals, but also tell them how to achieve them, in a way that destroys the enthusiasm and creativity of your people?

6 Do you listen, *really* listen, to your team members?

7 Do your teams really move ideas, and how effective are your team's conversations? Are your conversations direct ones? Is everyone engaged in the conversation? Are the best ideas coming to the surface and are your teams grabbing them, and making them happen?

Hot teams in a cold climate

Norsk Hydro breaks the rules for a fast recovery in the face of adversity

The pursuit of heroic success and *big change* is characteristic of many of the virtuoso team examples that we've looked at in this book. This is a natural application for such teams because of their innate ability and inclination to break out of contemporary norms and rethink the business, the customer, or the organization. But, in some cases, a good recovery might be more important than a great initiative. In some instances, the future of the firm hangs on its ability to move on quickly after a near-disastrous stumble in a product market. Norsk Hydro, the large Norwegian firm with an interest in using its oil and energy business to build a global presence, offers us an unusually vivid example of how a true virtuoso group can be used to 'fix' a problem rather than launch a new beginning.

What we'll see in this chapter is how a team recovering from an unfortunate strategic choice can be as 'big' as a team creating a new product or entering a new market. At Norsk Hydro we'll see how, within a large and complex organization, hierarchy, title, and traditional job roles are put aside by senior executive sponsorship. Instead, senior leadership breaks through traditional organizational boundaries and makes real talent mobile through the creation of a virtuoso team to resolve significant corporate issues. Once the team is launched, we'll see how the team leader uses a combination of unreasonable time pressures and 'creative abrasion' (pairing strong egos in order to generate energy within a team) as a catalyst to a profoundly different way of teamwork. We'll also see that the personal and central involvement of the team leader, and a reliance on carefully choreographed weekly meetings, can be a particularly effective way to manage the big egos associated with virtuoso teams.

Norsk Hydro: a globally diverse organization

Norsk Hydro is one of the largest and best-known companies in Norway, occupying, at the time of this case, a major position in the offshore agricultural and aluminum products businesses, as well as being a major developer of oil wells. In 2003 it was a Fortune 500 company, operating in 40 countries. At the time of the incidents related in this chapter, Norsk Hydro had three divisions: Oil & Energy, Aluminum Products, and Agriculture. It employed 44,000 people and was listed on several equity markets. Hydro was originally founded in 1905, and entered the oil and energy business in the late 1970s. During the 1990s, in a bid to establish itself beyond the national wells in the Norwegian Sea, Hydro had gone to Angola, the Gulf of Mexico, and elsewhere, with high expectations of finding rich oil sources. With discoveries coming in rapid succession, particularly in offshore wells similar to those in Norway, Angola was seen as the 'hottest' place to be for the big oil companies.

Traditional exploration: driven by teams

Hydro's normal approach to oil exploration was to send an exploration team to a site with the long-term goal of 'finding opportunities' and hence with no immediate list of deliverables imposed on them. The typical Hydro exploration team covered several disciplines and included geochemists, geophysicists and engineers, who would stay together for three to five years, rarely mixing with the other teams due to the massive amounts of data they were working with: sifting through this data looking for clues, testing with computer simulations, trying to tease out indications of potential oil reserves. Typically, these teams were independent and self-contained, allowing them to address their projects in a fast and comprehensive fashion, but occasionally risking 'siloing.' The work of the exploration teams was considered both highly scientific and unpredictable.

First of all you need rock that contains the right content of organic remains, then you need rock that the hydrocarbons can flow into, and finally you need the right type of rock to prevent the hydrocarbons from flowing away. Geologists have been heard saying: 'Yes, there has been oil here, but we are a few million years too late.' And it's not just a question of finding the right kind of rock. It also has to be possible and profitable to produce the hydrocarbons it contains. All these factors provide interesting challenges for geologists and other scientists and engineers who work with oil and gas.

Seismic charting (which is central to the entire process of identifying and appraising potential oil reserves) involves sending sound waves down to the seabed and then registering the signals that are reflected back by the geological formations. These signals are processed in powerful computers, and the results are drawn up in a seismic chart. Geophysicists study this information to assess the geology of the area. The interpretation of oil and gas discoveries is difficult. Once a discovery is made, there are new questions to be answered. How big is it? How much of it can be produced? What will its lifetime be? These questions can only be properly answered if the seismic data is of top quality and interpretation technology is combined with a thorough understanding of geology.

In order to meet this daunting challenge, Norsk Hydro relied upon exploration teams, each of which had its own complete set of experts, and a high degree of autonomy. According to Knut Aanstad, Norsk Hydro's vice president for business development in the oil division: 'They are sent to go and evaluate data. It is hard to get quick results or set schedules.' The payoff for being on a winning team was high visibility within the company and, hence, opportunities for promotion. On the other hand, the risks inherent in 'inaccurate' assessments depended on the nature of the errors committed: at the extreme, if they included gross errors, careers could be at risk, though not if the errors were deemed to be within acceptable limitations of data interpretation.

The Bloc 34 experience: a future opportunity for global growth

During the 1990s, the waters off the coast of the west African country of Angola began to show great promise in the search for new oil reserves. On the heels of a multi-billion barrel offshore oil strike in what was locally referred to as 'Bloc 17,' the Angolan government decided to open large, uncharted areas nearby for bids and exploration by international oil companies. For the cost of production and exploratory drilling, these companies could share in the profits for years to come. Hydro, in its efforts to globalize, was extremely interested in participating in the Angolan prospects. In addition, as the representative of a small but independent nation, the Angolan authorities apparently favored Hydro as an exemplar from which a developing country could learn.

Of particular interest to the oil companies was a specific plot of offshore property that had been designated as 'Bloc 34.' In somewhat deeper waters on the Angolan continental shelf and adjoining Bloc 17, Bloc 34 was rated as an unusually good prospect. In preparation for a possible bid, Hydro sent a crack team of five scientists with the latest technologies to probe the site and, under the leadership of Erling Vagues, they spent four years evaluating it in secret.

According to Vagues: 'We looked at the data and eventually developed a consensus that [Bloc 34] was virtually certain to contain a huge reservoir of oil.' Furthermore, the experts of two of Hydro's potential partners reached nearly identical conclusions, which convinced the top managers to bid for drilling rights.

The seismic data in the virtual map the team had filled in, it appeared, was irrefutable: there was a very large reservoir of oil. Together, the three corporate partners placed a bid worth hundreds of millions of dollars, in addition to a promise to finance three drilling sites and the prospect of decades of profit, and subsequently won the right to exploit the site.

As vice-president for business development in the oil division, Knut Aanstad bore direct responsibility for overseeing Vagues' team. 'Bloc 34,' explained Aanstad, 'was seen as the jewel in the crown in Angola. We rated the probability of an oil strike at about 70%, when the odds are usually about 15% to 20%. It was a high profile deal and was presented as the cornerstone of our international expansion.' In many ways, Bloc 34 was projected to be one of the most valuable assets of Hydro's activities.

Bloc 34: the reality surprises everyone

On April 10, 2002, Aanstad received word, and it was bad. Bloc 34 had turned out to be dry. This was a huge blow: Hydro had not only invested a significant amount of money, but had also publicly trumpeted Bloc 34 as a major step in its evolution into a successful global oil company. Investor expectations were influenced by the predictions for Bloc 34. Moreover, this failure was the largest in a string of rather poor results that Hydro had recently experienced in similar exploration elsewhere. A major and immediate concern within the company was how the closely-watching investment community would receive this news. What would be the impact on Hydro's equity price and market valuation? How would the negative results at Bloc 34 affect morale throughout the company? In just a very short few months, investors and industry analysts would need to be informed about it honestly and openly, for Bloc 34 had been presented to them as a near-sure thing in what was otherwise a notoriously risky industry.

But, what to say? The trouble was that, in view of all the scientific indicators that had convinced Hydro and its partners that Bloc 34 would be a big oil strike, no one knew exactly what could have gone wrong. In ad-dition, it normally took a long time for Hydro experts, working in the traditional way, to evaluate and interpret available information. The delay that was to be expected for developing the reason for the failure would be, in and of itself, a strong and unacceptable message to be sent to the investment community. Finally, the exploratory team in the field was so deeply involved in the outcome and so demoralized at the recent results that they did not appear to be the best option to be relied upon for determining just what went wrong.

Bloc 34: the virtuoso team response

Faced with a possibly catastrophic situation, Norsk Hydro senior management decided that it could not afford to address this situation in a traditional way: too much was at stake, a novel response was needed, and time was of the essence. On the return flight home from Angola, three top Norsk Hydro executives – Knut Aanstad, his boss Morton Ruud (who reported directly to the Board of Directors) and Eigil Rasmussen (Ruud's special advisor on both scientific and business matters) – decided that a bold, rapid, and effective response was essential. They decided to create a high-powered task force, a true virtuoso team, made up of Hydro's best people, position by position, and give them an unusual level of freedom in which to work. They would have approximately six weeks to reinterpret the data, which would typically be regarded as an unreasonably short amount of time. In order to assemble this team, Ruud promised to get top-priority support from the company board, allowing Aanstad to put whoever he wanted on the team, with the authority to pull them from whatever tasks they were currently engaged in. This total circumvention of hierarchy and traditional ways of doing business was virtually unprecedented within Hydro, but then so was the urgency of the situation. The newly created virtuoso team would be given the mandate to reinterpret a stream of data so massive that it had occupied the minds of some of the best professionals in the company full time for over four years.

Obtaining a mandate to jump-start the team

Having gained a firm commitment from the top of the organization, Aanstad set about compiling a list of potential leaders and members for the team. It was to be composed of the best people in the company who had the required technical expertise. He could immediately call on anyone he chose, regardless of what they were working on and which division was their professional home. Because most of Hydro's experts worked almost exclusively within their assigned divisions, this represented a highly unusual grant of authority. Given the politics of the organization, it was also a delicate task: Aanstad had to avoid both advocates and opponents of the global expansion scheme; otherwise, he worried, he risked getting 'tainted advice' from an opinionated position rather than a scientifically objective reinterpretation of the data. In other words, members of the team had to have no direct institutional stakes in what they were investigating. Though rumors were circulating about the fate of Bloc 34, the team would work in total secrecy from the rest of the company.

The leader is chosen

With great care, Kjell Sunde was chosen to be the leader of the taskforce. He had had experience with similar projects: rather than being a traditional line manager, he was part of what was known within Hydro as the 'risk police;' an independent group that was frequently called in to evaluate and double-check drilling prospects at short notice and under great time pressure. Not surprisingly, Sunde was a generalist and accustomed to jumping quickly into projects in a non-political manner and hence was not beholden to any of the positions factions within the company. Though he had begun his career at Hydro as a typical geophysicist, he no longer spent years evaluating the data from any one drilling bloc. In terms of leadership style, Sunde viewed himself as a catalyst, that is, he believed that once the right people were found for the job they should be allowed to work more or less on their own, with some input from him but for the most part autonomously. If they were shown trust, Sunde reasoned, they would deliver better work than if someone was constantly looking over their shoulder. In a nutshell, he said, 'freedom motivates.'

Sunde was given the authority to choose anyone from Aanstad's list of potential team members and could add additional people if he deemed it necessary. Regarding the people he chose, Sunde remembered: 'It was a mix of technical brilliance and gut feeling on who would work well together.' Sunde knew that some of the team members had the reputation of being 'not easy.' They were supremely confident in their abilities, and hence always sought to dominate the teams that they were a part of; they also tended to seek the limelight aggressively, in an effort, some would say, to 'hog the credit.' Somehow, Sunde knew, he had to get this team of all-stars to work together. Not only did they thrive on recognition but they also needed to feel they were doing an outstanding job, part of which included leading (or dominating) others. 'I needed,' Sunde concluded, 'to inspire them and allow them exposure – to give credit where credit is due – yet at the same time to control how much and when.'

The team at work

Early on, Sunde realized that the tightness of the schedule could be a great asset: team members would be energized by the pressue and too busy to do anything other than concentrate on the tasks at hand. His challenge was to compress all the steps needed into the tight deadline. He organized the work around a series of weekly status meetings, at which taskforce members would sum up the status of their work and then open the floor for suggestions and criticism both in methodology and to identify gaps in information that other team members needed. At the conclusion of each meeting, Sunde and a colleague would then pull all of the information generated into an updated unified view. Such meetings would be totally open forums to challenge, support, and address the key issues in direct conversations. It was essential that title, politics, and politeness didn't dampen the effective flow of ideas.

In the kickoff meeting on April 17, Sunde stressed that the team was not looking to place blame, but rather to find a sound, fact-based, explanation for what had happened. It was a way, he said, to move ahead. This vision was an effort to set a positive tone and focus the task for the team, while at the same time allaying the anxieties of the original team in the field, who would be called upon to provide raw data and explain their original assumptions.

The morale of Sunde's team was high, even if they were somewhat anxious about the magnitude of the task before them. To be picked for the project, they all knew, was a clear acknowledgment of membership in the elite of the company ('the "A" Team,' as it was called by some). It was a sign of trust in their abilities to perform outstanding work in a pressure-cooker environment on what seemed to be an impossible task. For the most part, they knew each other already, which eliminated the need to build polite relationships, and which enabled them to jump in and get started right away. Though they did not give themselves an official name, they joked that they were not a taskforce but 'forced to task.' Their work, Sunde emphasized, would take place autonomously from the rest of the company. There would be no micro-management and no intrusive scrutiny from above and yet, as signaled by a memo from Ruud, they had absolute top priority and access to any resources they required; there were to be no barriers to their speedy and successful conclusion of this project. Finally, it was understood by all that to satisfy investors and industry analysts, their conclusions had to be definitive and leave no room for debate or second-guessing.

Close quarters: dancing to the rhythm

Because half of the team came from outside Oslo headquarters, Sunde set up a dedicated room for them, including computer workstations and other necessary scientific and communications equipment. The space was nothing fancy, but it functioned as a common meeting place for both problem solving and – in the few moments they had to spare – some socializing. Members of the team were going to spend huge amounts of time together – up to 90 hours per week – often taking their meals at their desks and occasionally going out for drinks later in the evening to wind down. The atmosphere in the room was relaxed and informal, which encouraged discussions that were open, honest and passionate. Given that the team assembled a number of big egos in a small space, there was plenty of friction and some early clashes, but the deadline pressure was so great that members had to maintain focus on the task at hand. They were all, as

Aanstad put it: 'aware that they needed to dance to the same rhythm.' Moreover, in view of the Norwegian style of 'balancing the needs of the individual with the group,' they strove to avoid explosive confrontations and personal anger. According to Sunde, team members were so dedicated that he felt that there was no need to manipulate or trick them into working harder.

Provoking interaction rather than directing the details

Sunde made himself totally available to answer questions and provide perspective when called upon by any team members, but he took a decidedly low-key role otherwise. After dividing the team into their respective disciplines, Sunde left them largely on their own to self-organize along the lines of their strengths and weaknesses. For example, according to Bard Krokan, Hydro's research and technology chief: 'The top geophysicists were put together. Sunde helped them by supplying their overall goals and asking them questions but it was more or less up to them how to get there. They quickly found what each could do best and divided their tasks optimally [on the] different parts of the problem.'

For his part, Sunde set deadlines and framed the problem – it was largely looking at data in retrospect rather than exploring some unproven potential, which simplified the task somewhat – but that was about all. 'We had to get from A to Z,' he explained, 'but I didn't care if they skipped B and went all the way to K. They knew what they were doing.' In posing the 'right questions,' Sunde would ask his team about a range of subjects, from the assumptions they were making when they cut corners due to lack of data to how they organized their time. However, he emphasized, the questions were meant to stimulate them to find their own solutions rather than direct them to a predetermined outcome that he as leader had in mind.

In spite of his hands-off management style, Sunde strove to engineer certain structures into the daily routines. First, in accordance with both their expertise and his intuitive sense of psychological fit, Sunde 'paired' team members to work together on certain 'critical elements': they were to work on related, though separate, problems. In that way, he explained, 'they would continually interact, bouncing ideas off each other and to a degree competing, or at least keeping their eyes on each other.' It was the best way, he believed, to promote objectivity and raise quality; however, these teams were not designed to promote personal confrontations: friction was supposed to be minimal and entirely directed at a passionate attack on their problems. Second, while they 'owned' a portion of the problem, Sunde wanted to make sure that they all identified their individual success with that of the group. In other words, each part had to fit with the others. This meant not only that the team members had to keep in mind an overview of the entire process but also that as the team leader, he had to avoid allowing an entrenched sense of ownership to develop for each separate problem, which would result, in his view, in hardened points of view, involving considerable egos, that would interfere with the ability of the team as a whole in successfully achieving its overall goals. All in all, he recognized that there was an extremely delicate balance that needed to be struck.

The weekly meetings

The first step in getting the team to work was to gather, scan, and interpret available information. Old reports had to be reviewed and Vagues' original team had to be interviewed. This was a delicate process because it could be seen as judging the original Bloc 34 team's initial, and upbeat, forecasts. One of the original team members said that the interviews, 'left them feeling run over by a steam roller,' as it made them feel forced onto the sidelines after four years of devoted effort. Vagues was concerned and worried that Sunde's powerhouse team would discover errors that he and his colleagues had overlooked in his approach. But he understood that the 'fresh eye' approach and information search by the taskforce was useful and necessary. 'It was agonizing,' Vagues related, 'but I sensed that the group had such great talent that it was set to erupt with creativity. We were prepared to cooperate fully.' Though some new experimental data was requested, such as water samples from the empty well, it was quickly concluded that not much more new data was required.

Once the initial data was gathered, the principal discipline that Sunde imposed upon his virtuosos was the weekly meeting. At this meeting, team members were asked to summarize their findings, understandings and needs, as they currently stood, conveying them formally in PowerPoint presentations. In an effort to use time most efficiently, the discussions were strictly limited to 15 minutes per presentation. As a result of this strict time discipline, Sunde expected that team members would use their brief moment to maximum effect; this would also, he reasoned, prevent the more aggressive members of the team from imposing their will or points of view on the others. Furthermore, because he did not announce the exact schedule for the meetings until the day before, team members could not plan for them over too long a period of time. There was no scheduling chart or indeed any physical indicators of all the individual tasks to accomplish.

Not all meetings are created equal. Sunde leveraged meetings to create a particularly well-thought-out way to drive the team forward. The meeting's predictability and unwavering format set a hard and fast deadline to which Sunde's team members had to respond. The meeting structure served as the focal point of the project and forged a sense of mutual ownership. In particular, the meetings revealed gaps in the process by finding out what issues the specialists were missing or where collaboration between specialists was essential. By helping to pinpoint who needed what piece of the information puzzle and when they needed it, the meetings served as a central repository of active knowledge exchange for the team. As an example, because certain types of geophysical data had to be made available to geochemists before the latter could proceed with their analyses, Sunde redeployed resources and sought additional input from available experts at the company in order to fill this gap. Moreover, when the team had to cut corners – making assumptions when they would normally rely on harder data and more exhaustive analyses – the entire team was made aware of the risks that this presented and correspondingly recalibrated their numbers to adjust. The meetings also served, Sunde explained, as a vehicle for him to guide the team when necessary: all members of the taskforce knew what they had to deliver and when.

The team members, however, saw these meetings as an extra burden they had to bear and complained about them often, mostly to each other. The environment, they argued, was already very stressful and they did not need to add to it an unnecessary ritual. In spite of these reservations, Sunde realized the discipline of the meetings was essential and he maintained them until the final weeks, when the sub-teams had to finalize their interpretations. In part, because in this phase the team members had to answer increasingly technical questions among experts, there were fewer meetings held during the last two weeks.

Results of the 'A' Team

The team was so busy that the chemistry among members had little chance, nor was it anyone's intention, to evolve or change much throughout the six weeks of the project. In fact, aside from the demands of the space and meeting requirements, the team members related to each other in more or less the same way that they had from the beginning – as individual virtuosos. This meant that Sunde's initial judgments regarding membership were of absolutely crucial importance to the working of the team. In order to meet the deadlines, they simply had to get along and work well together from day one.

With one week to go, team members made their final presentations to Sunde and then handed over their PowerPoint slides, which Sunde and a trusted colleague incorporated into their final report. The project was over and a rough consensus had been reached in which there was no substantial disagreement amongst team members. Their conclusion was that:

1. the original team had made no gross errors, but instead had done exactly what they were supposed to do;

2. the mistaken assessment had arisen from a 'gas residue' that created the appearance of an oil reservoir.

These conclusions were presented to investors and stock analysts on Norsk Hydro's 'capital market day' at the end of July. The stakes as to how this would be received were extremely high. If investors or analysts were unconvinced by the presentation, or felt that Hydro was hiding something, they might lose confidence in the firm and conceivably downgrade the stock, perhaps significantly. Though it would be an exaggeration to say that the survival of the company was at stake, the impact could nonetheless be heavy. Furthermore, Hydro's partners in Angola also needed to be satisfied with the explanation, if there was to be a possibility for future collaborative explorations.

Virtually everyone connected with the project was impressed with how quickly and accurately the reassessment had been accomplished. 'I was astonished,' Ruud recalled, 'at how such a large and complex interdisciplinary problem could be solved so quickly. They could easily have spent a year on this and not even get results that were this good . . . Cost wasn't an issue in this case, but in fact it was much cheaper to do it this way,' that is, more efficient in terms of manpower and talent utilization. Krokan was deeply impressed as well. 'I learned,' he said, 'that you can put the best people together, give them lots of autonomy, and get to the goal without conflict and without hidden agendas. It was amazing.' One of the questions that Ruud and other managers began to ask themselves was why they could not achieve results like those of the taskforce all the time.

Despite the success of the team, its élite nature worried some managers. As Ruud put it: 'I liked the way that the team shook things up. It injected a bit of instability into the organization that was useful. But it was also threatening to rank and file employees. I don't want to create an "A" Team because that means that there is also a "B" Team. That would be bad for morale.' Krokan agreed yet thought that more junior employees with high potential might benefit from inclusion in similar team assignments, perhaps using them as a training ground: 'We could throw them in where the learning curve is the steepest,' he explained. 'We might even be able to develop some new taskforce group every year [in which] older employees could share their experience with their younger colleagues.'

Implications for leading virtuoso teams: Summary and Key Questions

Norsk Hydro's use of a virtuoso team is an excellent example of where a firm recognizes the significance of the challenge that it faces, appreciates the need for fast and effective action, and resolves to do whatever it takes to achieve a successful recovery. We believe that once Knut Aanstad received approval to select the best talent obtainable, no matter where in the company they were located, and no matter what they were working on at that moment, Norsk Hydro's Bloc 34 'A' team was a real virtuoso team. Furthermore, once it was assembled, the appointment of Kjell Sunde as team leader was a clear signal that this talent was not to be squandered, and Sunde responded appropriately with a management style that both focused the team's objective and yet allowed the talent to run with its own head in a way that gave it the maximum opportunity to really fulfill its potential.

Meetings need not be boring or just for 'information purposes.' In fact they can be vital levers leaders can use to drive virtuoso teams forward. Aanstad's creativity illustrates how face-to-face dialog in a weekly team meeting, is effective to coordinate work, test hypotheses, raise key questions, and exchange ideas and knowhow between high performers operating under pressure.

In between meetings, Sunde's leadership style was to relax constraints on the team, which resulted in loose control over how the virtuosos did their work. We see again and again how effective virtuoso leaders combine such tight and loose control over teams. Tight controls to make sure experts exchange views and coordinate effectively to move the total project forward. Loose controls to avoid micro-management, which is totally counterproductive when talented people are available. Sunde was able to extract high performance from his collection of virtuosos. Senior management provided important cover for the team as well. By separating the team from the organization and its associated culture, traditions, and rules, Sunde was able to put his own personal leadership stamp and philosophy into play without managerial interference.

By invoking many principles from virtuoso teams we have studied, the Bloc 34 case raises some important questions for all managers interested in harnessing the élite talent available in their firm:

1   When faced with really big opportunities – or as in the case of Bloc 34, challenges – is your firm able to wrest itself from its typical approach to launching projects and creating teams, put these aside, and quickly configure top leadership and talent into a virtuoso team of your most talented performers?

2   Do your virtuoso leaders understand the need of instilling teamwork based on elements of discipline and routine, even if resistance sets in, to accomplish vital knowledge exchange among the experts? Do they understand discipline, such as the weekly meetings at Hydro, making sure the expert views are brought together, face-to-face, on a regular basis and without fail – to openly and directly share opinions and views to keep the overall project on track?

3   Do your virtuoso team leaders understand that in addition to discipline, freedom is also a hallmark of a high-performing virtuoso team? Do your leaders allow the freedom needed to unleash talent, by not interfering with the day-to-day work of the virtuoso performers?

4   Are goals, objectives, and constraints clearly understood by each virtuoso team member? Does each team member know how their expertise fits into these goals and objectives?

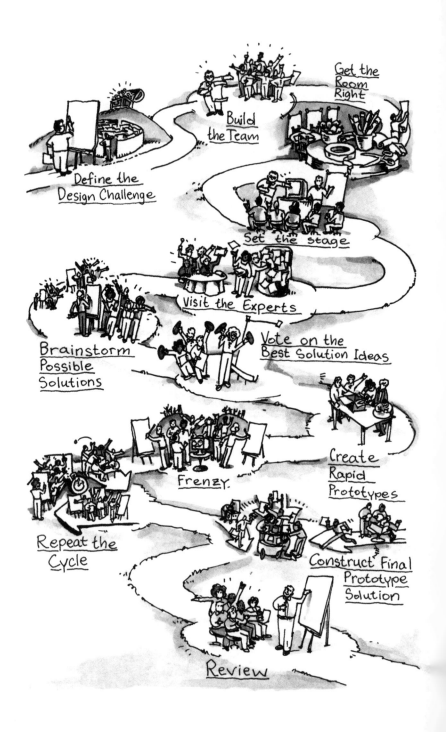

9
Turbo-charge your own team

How you can lead your team for high performance

As we've seen throughout this book, creating and leading virtuoso teams can be a daunting challenge. Trying to get the very best talent to work together can be extremely difficult. In fact, the very act of being able to identify and attract the very best talent is a luxury that many managers are unable to enjoy. Instead, most of us inherit the teams that we have to work with, or we simply can't staff our teams with the very best people obtainable. Complex and opaque organizational environments might even make it difficult for us to identify who the best people are. Clearly, in such situations to even speak of 'virtuoso teams' can be a stretch. More often than not, it's 'who's available' rather than 'who's obtainable' that we have to work with. We believe, however, that even typical teams can achieve virtuoso results, when the conditions are right.

To begin with, we subscribe to the belief that most typical teams, while not populated with 'all-stars,' nonetheless include skilled professionals who are dedicated, talented, and energetic, and all too often looking for a chance to show their talent. Yet, as we've stressed throughout this book, individual talent alone is not sufficient to ensure high team performance. Achieving high performance is elusive for typical teams as well as for virtuoso performers. The real questions become: 'Is there a way to turbo-charge almost any team to achieve higher performance?' 'What should a team do to approach virtuoso-type performance?' 'What management lessons can we learn from virtuoso teams that we can apply to typical teams?'

Drawing from our research and experience with firms in many cultures and industries, we have developed a systematic process that can serve as a catalyst to higher team performance. It involves many of the same characteristics that we've seen in the virtuoso teams in this book, namely:

> speed;
>
> respect for individual talent;
>
> pushing for clear goals and objectives;
>
> boldness and risk-taking;
>
> strong leadership roles;
>
> direct dialog with intense conversation;
>
> prototyping and learning from failure and;
>
> several other aspects of virtuoso teams that you'll recognize as we go along.

We believe that the process is effective for teams facing a wide variety of opportunities and challenges that range from crafting new strategies and redesigning organizations, to developing new values or customer promises. In fact, one fast-moving consumer goods firm is presently using this process to jump-start all teams launching new projects, aimed at supporting a major transformation across an entire region. Another global telecom network operator has employed the approach to design a performance management system for all of its employees.

DeepDive*

We call this process DeepDive. In this chapter you will learn what DeepDive is, and how and why it works. You'll also learn how to use the DeepDives in your company, with your own teams. We believe the DeepDive, and the elements of the process, can help any manager in any type of organization, even if they have no hope of creating true virtuoso teams. The discussion of the DeepDive will also illustrate several important lessons for managers about achieving virtuoso team performance, goal setting, prototyping, brainstorming, effective conversations, learning, team selection, and getting expert views. The DeepDive process manages these elements explicitly, but all managers can keep them in mind to be applied to any team, whether they are using the process or not.

The importance of **really** managing teams

With so many projects underway and so many different teams working busily, it's frequently difficult for management to know what is going on inside those teams, and to ensure their high performance. How can management be confident that the teams are getting the most from their talent? That they are focused clearly on goals and objectives? That the leadership of those teams is effective? If the answers to these questions are simply more questions, then perhaps it is time to rethink how teamwork is being done in your organization. Ironically, no company that we work with would ever be so casual about how they manage cash flow, materials flow, customer information flow, or the use of their brand and logos. So, why then are

---

* DeepDive is a trademark of DeepDive Products™ 2005. All rights reserved. For more information go to **www.deepdive-production.com**.

so many organizations so casual about how their team-based talent, often the backbone of key initiatives and projects in an organization, is working and being led? We offer the DeepDive as one tool you can use to better understand how to 'virtuoso-ize' your teams, not just on *one* project, but on project after project after project.

We all know not to micro-manage, but too often the leader is left on their own, to draw from their own skills, knowledge, and experiences, to move their teams. Even if each leader is well-intentioned, the results will undoubtedly be procedurally diverse, with occasionally random approaches to teamwork and project management. That's not acceptable, given the importance of getting the most out of a team's talent. Some teams may by chance have a collection of people that have good chemistry together, while other teams, again by luck of the draw, have bad chemistry. Whatever the exact situation is, the quality of the teamwork can vary widely and, as a result, the quality of the projects or initiatives will also vary widely. The implications for strategy, change, and driving progress in the firm can be significant. Managers may not be aware of what is happening in the teams or why some work and others don't. There is no way to systematically improve the teams, or to improve the way that they work. After all, there is no process. The consequence is important. Envisioned strategies and changes fall short of the mark. The people on the teams may be happy, but the results may be mediocre. Clearly then, getting teams energized and effective is an important move.

The first step to getting the most out of your teams is to manage them as carefully as you would other critical activities in the firm. The DeepDive helps organizations move in this direction, and it also helps managers understand and emulate some fundamentals of great teams.

The birth of the DeepDive as a process for managerial teamwork

Our first exposure to some of the core elements of the DeepDive came from an unlikely source. On an Executive MBA tour to Silicon Valley, we found ourselves watching an extraordinary ABC *Nightline News* video illustrating how a leading product, service and experience design firm, named IDEO, actually did its teamwork. The video, showing the firm designing a supermarket shopping cart, was just the portal to a deep treasure chest of intriguing managerial concepts we discovered at IDEO. The firm turned out to be a hothouse of interesting people and ideas about how to get the most out of teams of talented individuals. IDEO provided a wealth of insights for a combination of reasons: the philosophy of management held by their founder, Dave Kelley, that aims at unleashing knowledge pro- fessionals and their potential; their proximity to Silicon Valley and the whirlwind of ideas, technology, and consumer concepts in play there; and that IDEO is in the basic business of moving ideas quickly, from consumer insights and concept through market consummation.

We then combined the key concepts that we saw at IDEO with our previous research and experience as executive development teachers/consultants. By blending these two different knowledge domains, we began to teach differently and work with teams differently in our executive program experiences at IMD. Over time, this marriage of different disciplines and perspectives gave birth to the initial formulation of the managerial DeepDive process as a way to drive virtuoso-like high performance teamwork in almost any situation.

The real breakthrough was the realization that the teams we studied in our typical managerial settings *mirrored the same fundamental issues* faced by IDEO's product design teams. In each instance, their teams and our management teams were essentially required to *design the best solution possible within certain constraints, to do this fast and to offer sufficient novelty in their solutions so as to overcome otherwise intractable problems.* Furthermore, these solutions were expected to not only be novel, but to work in a practical manner, as well.

What we saw at IDEO, however, was a process that really got the most out of the talent deployed on teams. It was a process that moved many and good ideas quickly, and allowed teams to take risks without necessarily being at risk. We think of the DeepDive as giving a team 'fast traction' on specific challenges and creating a very focused conversation with intense idea flow.

Our objective in this chapter is to describe the process and its logic, so that you and managers like yourself can use the DeepDive to turbo-charge your teams, facing a whole host of managerial challenges, towards virtuoso performance.

THE POWER OF A DEEPDIVE LIES IN ITS ABILITY TO:

* Concentrate the attention of a management team on a specific company challenge

* Put the team under considerable time pressure – which has the effect of eliminating unnecessary behaviors that frustrate innovation and problem solving

* Create explicitly high expectations for results

* Encourage ideas outside the norm

* Encourage building on the ideas of others

* Use rapid prototyping: failing early and often to succeed sooner

* Energize conversations about the key issues the team faces

* Use time very efficiently to get results fast

Projects and teamwork: emerging as strategic capabilities

Let's step back for a moment and understand the role that teams have in most organizations today. Teams are crucial to business success. Whether designing new products, planning entry to a new market, responding to the competition, or even developing people to their highest potential, managerial work today is reaching new levels of complexity. Challenges such as these can only be met by leveraging the intellect, energy, and creativity of many people with varying perspectives – in other words, by using teams. Most firms rely on teams to break down silos that inhibit idea flow, collaboration, innovation and change. Traditional firms, steeped in hierarchy, may be efficient, consistent, predictable, and reliable, but typically they are not innovative, adaptive, flexible, market responsive or technologically inventive. Teams are a vital tool managers use to augment traditional methods and add important capabilities to organizations. They short-circuit the 'disconnects' that plague so many traditional companies. In fact, for these reasons, teams are increasingly the primary engine of performance for many of today's most respected organizations.[1]

Unfortunately, not all teams are created equal, and not all are effective, resulting in lost opportunities and ultimately a huge bottom-line impact. Frustration with team performance has driven many companies to alternative 'quick-fix' solutions – bringing in consultants, training people in facilitation and meeting-management skills, making improvements in facilities and technology. While such 'quick fix' solutions have their own merit, they fundamentally address symptoms rather than pathologies; 'hygiene' factors rather than what it really takes to reliably get great teamwork. Giving a team the latest computing technology, an agenda, a facilitator, a timekeeper, a leader, and a sense of mutual respect is no guarantee that they will produce results. Most of these techniques and products can help a team get off the ground, and might be able to transform bad teamwork into good – but what about taking these good results further – to make them *great*?

What amazes us is that despite the big potential paybacks involved (for high-performing teams produce far better results than average ones), truly high-performing teams are

---

1 Katzenbach, Jon R. and Smith, Douglas, K. *The Wisdom of Teams*. McGraw-Hill, 1993, p. 5.

rare.[2] Even rarer, however, is to discover an organization which has established a system, or process, for improving teamwork; for taking team performance seriously. Consider the possible corporate return on the total investment made in teams. In most organiz-ations that we are familiar with, there is a distribution of outcomes associated with teamwork: a few are great, many are reasonably good, and some are awful! This means two things: first, anything that can shift the performance of *all* teams to the right (higher performance) would be valuable; and second, the best way to dramatically increase any company's return on team investment is to find a way to have more teams entering into the *great* category. Well-led virtuoso teams, by definition, have performance way out on the right-hand side of the distribution; but those teams are really only appropriate for truly strategic initiatives. There are many more teams in an organization that are doing day-to-day work, for when, finding ways to move the distribution to the right is of extraordinary value.

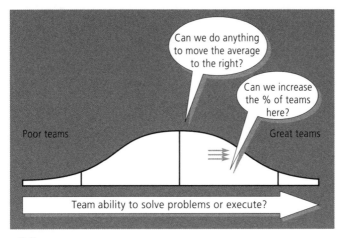

The DeepDive is a process and a discipline that radically accelerates the ability of teams to perform. The DeepDive spurs teams to higher performance – immediately directing all the team's energies at delivering results, fast. Compare that to the usual cycle of 'forming, storming, norming, and performing,' where days or weeks can be consumed before a single new idea is generated.

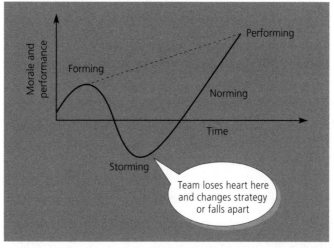

Source: www.businessballs.com/tuckmanformingstormingnormingperforming.htm – the model is by Bruce Tuckman, who in 1965 coined the "forming, storming, norming, and performing" phases, in that order [see also www.infed.org/thinkers/tuckman.htm]. He later added "adjourning" as the fifth phase. Katzenback and Smith use a version of this in Katzenback, Jon R. and Smith, Douglas K. *The Wisdom of Teams*, London: McGraw Hill, 1993, p. 84.

It's not enough, of course, for a single team to achieve results. The DeepDive, as a process and a discipline, enables you to improve the performance of teams across your company. After all, *knowledge-based industries are at the early stages of a revolution that will radically improve the returns of team-based work, the same way that industrial engineering and mass production (both of which are process-based) greatly increased the returns from manufacturing;* what they now need is processes appropriate to knowledge work.

This is not just our view – but rather something we've learned from the managers we've worked with. We've applied the DeepDive, with great results, to businesses ranging from telecoms to engineering services, from manufacturing to international aid, in solving challenges ranging from strategic planning to kicking off new organizations, driving commercial results, and perfecting communication and coordination within the firm.

An overview of the process

What exactly is a DeepDive? It's a focused team approach to develop solutions for specific challenges. It is intended to harness the idea-power of everyone on a team in a directed, creative, and energizing way. A DeepDive is a time-constrained combination of brainstorming, prototyping, and feedback loops melded together into an approach that any manager can use.

A DeepDive can be done in as little as half a day, or the process can be used to achieve results over a longer period. A sketch of the typical steps follows.

First, formulate a clear and well-articulated design challenge. What is the issue you want to solve? That should be the objective of your DeepDive. Try to state it in one sentence. Every good design challenge includes constraints – these are the characteristics that the solution will have to meet in order to be a success. For example, a constraint might be meaningful and measurable results within a specified timeframe. Another might be cost. With a well- formulated challenge, including clear constraints, you achieve a marriage between creativity and realism – innovative solutions that will work.

Second, build the team. Selecting team members is a key success factor. Look for a mix of skills and experiences. Typically you'd have three to four teams of four to eight people.

Third, get the room right. Make sure you set up an environment that lends itself to creativity. Things like posters, snacks, toys, and open space all help.

Once you have the challenge, the team, and the space, it's time to set the stage. The team needs some basic training on the DeepDive approach, and ideally to observe a DeepDive in action – here the IDEO video is very useful.[3]

The team's first step after the launch is to gather ideas and identify key issues by immersing themselves quickly in the topic. They do this by interacting with experts who, depending on the situation, might be team members or people external to the team. The goal is to understand and share all the key issues across the group, so that there's a good starting point for developing solutions.

Then, it's to the heart of the DeepDive: a series of brainstorming- prototyping-frenzy cycles that generate progressively superior solutions. Start with the DeepDive form of brainstorming to generate and capture lots of ideas

3 ABC News, 'Nightline: The Deep Dive,' July 13, 2003, www.abcnewsstore.com

and solutions to the issues identified. The 'rules' for effective brainstorming, which are included in the process, are key to making this work. The rules are:

▌ defer judgement

▌ encourage wild ideas

▌ build on the ideas of others

▌ stay focused on topic

▌ one conversation at a time

▌ be visual

▌ go for quantity

Source: IDEO

The more ideas generated, the better: quantity is better than quality at this point. Each team then selects a few promising ideas for testing, and very quickly builds a prototype. The emphasis should be on 'quick' here. We want to set a cadence for working fast and testing ideas fast. All of the teams will test their prototypes in a real-time 'frenzy' that sees each team showing-off their ideas and gathering feedback from the other teams and experts. This fast testing of ideas provides a powerful dose of reality early in the idea-formulation stage, preventing a team from wasting their time on ideas that have no future. After getting feedback on their prototype, each team enters into another brainstorming-rapid prototyping-frenzy cycle. These cycles can be repeated as often as needed or as time permits.

A prototype can take almost any form: it can be a physical object, a poster, a framework, a drawing, a description, a script, a list, even a sketch or role-play. The idea is to represent the desired solution with as much realism as possible. This makes the *implicit, explicit*. Focus on key elements of the design challenge in the prototype, rather than trying to prototype the entire solution. The fast pace and energy level is critical for success; less can really be more at this stage, as having too much time can result in the team becoming bogged down in unnecessary detail.

Having built a prototype, the team needs to get constructive and honest feedback. While prototypes need to be as concrete as possible, they (even the final prototype) are not the right answer! That is exactly the point – the prototypes are created in the spirit of 'failing to learn'.

Prototypes are a rapid learning device; and that means that when prototypes are displayed for feedback, it is not appropriate to defend them or explain how the team designed them. At this stage, what's important is just to get as much feedback as possible – which means listening, not explaining or defending or debating. Keep in mind that since prototypes are never 'right' or 'finished,' they are a license to fail. Take advantage of this license and aim for bolder prototypes. The inevitable compromises will always come later, and there is little to be gained by having compromises on top of compromises.

When the team has heard all the feedback, it's time to move to the next prototyping cycle. This takes a discipline that is not typical, since the natural human response will be to explain why the feedback is incorrect or unfair. The team needs to forget that and collect learning from the frenzy, and then quickly build another prototype which incorporates the best points from the team's previous work *and* from the feedback it just received. Time pressure – at times wildly unrealistic time pressure – is the catalyst that gets this to happen. The DeepDive is conducted around cycles of brainstorming (idea generation), rapid prototyping (build solutions), and frenzies (feedback) can be best orchestrated for maximum effect. See Appendix 2 for some examples of agendas and design challenges.

A facilitator can play a key role in this phase. Each team will naturally want to refine its idea as much as possible, and will be reluctant to go for more feedback until the next prototype is 'perfected'. This is a mistake; more learning occurs during the feedback cycle than during any other phase of the process! The facilitator's job is to push the teams to be bold and daring with their ideas, go for as much feedback as possible, and accept the feedback without explaining or getting defensive.

Once a few cycles have been completed, the teams will have generated a large number of 'prototype' solutions. In the final frenzy, it's a good idea to include an outside authority – which might be the team's facilitator, or a corporate executive – to provide some input for helping the teams select which prototypes or aspects look most promising. The intent is not to second-guess the teams, but rather to provide some outside perspective.

With this input, and another visit with the experts if desired, the team builds a final prototype which captures the best elements of all the previous trials and of the feedback they have collected. This final prototype is shared with the target audience and becomes the basis for the solution to the challenge that triggered the DeepDive.

The final step should be a review of the DeepDive, to capture all the ideas and inputs about how the process worked and what you'd like to do differently next time. This After Action Review[4] should involve everyone that took part – the team members and the target audience.

A more complete description of the process steps is found in Appendix 1. You'll notice that steps 1–4 address a lot of the issues you'll need to consider when you're planning a DeepDive, steps 4–11 deal with actually leading the process, and step 12 is the review. We recommend that you look at all the steps at once, and refer to the appropriate sections while you're planning or running your DeepDive.

Following our summary of each step we have gone 'in-depth' and highlighted several steps of the process that are essential to turbo-charging your teams.

Key process elements: key considerations to jump-start DeepDives in your organization

The DeepDive process is an attempt at gaining virtuoso team performance from any group on a more reliable basis. As our research into such great virtuoso teams as Edison's Muckers, or the team that created *West Side*

4 The After Action Review (AAR) is a technique for learning used by the US Army and was brought to our attention by Professor David Garvin, Harvard Business School, who translated the AAR into a powerful mangerial and organizational learning process. See David A. Garvin, *Learning In Action: A Guide to Putting the Learning Organization to Work*, Cambridge, Harvard Business School Press, 2003.

Story, or Amundsen's team that discovered the South Pole, illustrates – attention to the details around how the team would work together was a hallmark of their success. Whether it was how they selected talent, crafted a vision, shared ideas and expertise, combined different talents into effective collaboration, or effectively utilized space; the virtuoso teams we studied paid attention to these details to achieve high performance. The DeepDive is a process that enables a leader and a team to achieve many of these same characteristics, but an important lesson from this book is that these details are of critical importance and cannot be left to chance!

To help professionals or managers launch the process in your organization, we next provide you with detailed suggestions for the four steps that are particularly critical to any effective DeepDive. Even though all components of the process are important, in our experience these four steps emerge as being particularly relevant for achieving successful DeepDives, and also highlight key lessons around effective teamwork. The four steps are:

1. defining the design challenge;
2. building the team;
3. rapid prototyping and;
4. conducting the learning frenzy.

We think that it goes without saying that since this is a team-based activity, at the heart of any great team performance is the selection of the talent that will be involved, and then ensuring that all their brainpower and energy are focused towards clear objectives, goals, or a vision. In the DeepDive, this is accomplished through the design challenge and team-building stages of the process. Two other features of very effective teams are a bias towards action and ensuring intense ongoing learning from doing and testing. Both of these elements are instilled into the DeepDive during the prototyping and learning frenzy steps of the process. With this in mind, we'll go in-depth into the four essential elements of a great DeepDive.

1. Define the design challenge: get the team focused and all on the same page

The DeepDive puts your team (and you) under considerable time pressure. This time pressure is actually desirable, since it will: set a cadence for the work, raise the energy level of the group and expectations about performance, promote good teamwork (against the 'common enemy,' the clock), and encourage directness and honesty (as there won't be time for people to consider the personal or political implications of their recommendations). However, all of these positive things will only happen if you give the teams a crystal-clear challenge to work on. If the challenge statement is not clear, you will find that the teams will instead spend most of their time trying to figure out what they are supposed to be doing, creating their own interpretations of the charge, and probably getting quite frustrated before they ask for help.

So – you need to create a *clear, simple, concise* design challenge for your teams to work on. The challenge should probably be a single sentence. It should be prominently featured in your introduction and posted on the walls in your plenary session and in the sub-team work areas. The challenge should be specific enough that people can tell whether it has been met by a prototype solution and, like any good objective, it should describe the required output and timing.

Let's take an example. Let's say that your company is trying to figure out how to drive sales of a critical new product line, which appears promising but has not been ramping up sales as quickly as you would like. The design challenge might be, '*Create a sales plan that will help drive sales of our new Delta product, targeting new sales of at least $40M within the next 12 months.*' This is a good design challenge; it is concise, clear, and precise enough to give the teams a clear objective without being too constraining.

What are some examples of less effective design challenges? Well, consider the following attempts to target the same challenge.

> '*Quickly increase the sales of the Delta product.*' This gets at the basic idea, but is not specific nor associated with a timeframe, so it might not provide enough focus for the teams, and might encourage them to spend a lot of time debating what the objective could or should be rather than designing solutions.

> '*Redesign the sales compensation system to encourage people to sell more of the Delta product.*' The trouble here is that instead of a challenge statement, this looks more like part of a potential solution. Also, there's no specific target for sales or timeframes, so it would be hard to tell whether a given solution met the objective.

'Make Delta our biggest-selling product by the end of this next fiscal year, and increase Delta's brand image in the market so that we exceed the sales achieved by OtherCo's Gamma product in the same time period.' While this challenge is quite clear, it is perhaps too broad – is the outcome really within the team's control? Teams trying to address this challenge will need to spend a lot of time finding and considering information that is not already in their heads or easy to get, such as the sales of their own and competitive product lines. This might encourage them to go off in separate directions rather than working together.

Furthermore, while allowing scope for innovative solutions, this challenge still limits the possible prototypes too much. For example, what if the Delta product could be sold through a distributor that doesn't care about the brand recognition?

One key to setting a good design challenge is thinking through what the appropriate constraints should be. This draws some limits around possible solutions and helps ensure that they are practical and usable.

A typical constraint would be to ask for: 'meaningful and measurable results within one year or less.' Be specific about the time, and make sure the solution delivers quickly (i.e. one year might be too long). 'Meaningful and measurable' implies that it can be implemented on a wide scale within the constraint time horizon. It's probably also a good idea to have a constraint such as: 'within the prevailing financial realities of your organization.' Again, you want creativity, but creativity that can become reality. On the other hand, you probably wouldn't want a constraint about: 'prevailing political or organizational realities' because those could be just the things you need to alter for meaningful change to occur.

In our example, '***Create a sales plan that will help drive sales of our new Delta product, targeting new sales of at least \$40M within the next 12 months***', the constraints are: working with the existing product, a 12 month timeframe, and a sales target. These constraints effectively make sure you know when you've come up with a workable solution.

You're probably getting the impression that setting the design challenge appropriately is one of the most important things you can do to get a good result from your DeepDive. You're absolutely right! Spend some time on this, try different definitions and wording, and ask some colleagues to give you feedback before the DeepDive on the clear, specific, concise challenge you're posing. That way, your teams will be able to confidently enter the solution space right away, as opposed to puzzling over their target.

One final note. Since you'll be working with a number of sub-teams, you can decide whether you want them all to work on the same challenge *or* you can have each sub-team work on a different challenge. For a first DeepDive, it's easiest for all teams to work on the same challenge, because then when they're critiquing each other's prototypes, they're all well immersed in the topic. Nevertheless, if you'd like to examine several different dimensions with your DeepDive, you can assign each team a different challenge. For instance, Appendix 2 includes three examples of DeepDives that are aimed at getting a better understanding of the company's key processes. Each team was given a different process to research and describe to the rest of the teams. The topic was common but each team had a different challenge. In each DeepDive agenda, pay particular attention to the times allowed, the design challenge, and the constraints. The DeepDive is about putting pressure on teams to get to the big issues, in a focused way, very fast.

2. Build the team: get the right talent in place

To run a successful DeepDive, you need to *get the right people involved*, and to make sure you have *enough of their time* dedicated to the activity. Fortunately, this is not as difficult as it sounds, since the DeepDive is fast, flexible, and fun.

In order to build the team, you need to know what you're asking of them. A DeepDive may be conducted in as little as three to five hours, and certainly should be doable within a single day for most challenges. The ideal is to book a block of time where participants will not be disturbed and will be able to give the DeepDive full attention. However, it is also possible to do DeepDives in 60–90 minute blocks of time spread over as much as a week – for example, this might be suitable to an offsite event such as a training course or management retreat where other topics are being discussed. Doing this all at once is best, but break up the time if you need to, in order to get the right people. It's clearly better to have the right people with a more difficult timeline than to proceed with a DeepDive lacking essential input.

A good DeepDive needs both creativity and discipline. To get creativity, you'll need to involve as diverse a group of people as you possibly can, and in sufficient numbers that you can break them up into at least two (ideally three or more) teams.

Even more important than the timeline or the number of people is the expertise and skills of your team members. The DeepDive relies upon the '1+1=3' principle of high-performing teams: the combination of skills in the room can generate creative ideas that the individuals would not be able to come up with alone. Diversity in the team is good because it generates more resourceful and more creative ideas; and unlike more traditional processes the DeepDive creates a powerful environment where traditional barriers of organization and hierarchy can be set aside. This means that you should feel free to mix functions, cultures, organizational levels, and personalities. In fact, the more of these dimensions you can vary, the more powerful the team. It helps to have a good mix of highly creative 'ideas' people and others who have good ability to reflect upon and summarize concepts.

You also will need to include some strong experts in the specific topic (or 'design challenge') that you plan to attack. Depending on who they are, and on the number you have available, you could either seed your strongest subject matter experts throughout the teams, or keep them separate as 'consultants' in the early part of the process.

Who are the best experts? That all depends on the specific challenge you are trying to solve, but they are not necessarily the people with the highest rank or the most experience with your organization. For example, if you are trying to re-orient your company to being more customer-aware and less internally focused, the experts are probably frontline customer-facing people such as sales representatives and support staff – or better yet, can you bring in some actual customers? If you're trying to improve execution capabilities, the experts will be those who really understand execution; if working on product strategy, you might need a mix of marketing and technology gurus. The key point here is that expertise needs to be specific to the challenge, and sufficiently detailed and hands-on to keep the activity grounded in reality.

That said, you should not let the need for expertise limit the team diversity. For instance, in the above example of the customer orientation challenge, you would not want to invite only the sales and support teams (especially since you may want to change behaviors elsewhere in the company too). Nor do you want to end up with a group in which everyone has already been involved in the challenge in some way – you want people without a vested interest, and who can bring really fresh thinking to the issue. Invite a mix of sales, engineering, marketing, operations, and so on – any mix is fine as long as there are enough experts to ensure realistic solutions, and enough diversity to generate less obvious ideas.

You're probably wondering how many people you can or should attract to the party. Teams of four to six people will probably be able to generate a broad range of ideas, without getting in each other's way. Likewise, when you get to the frenzy stage, where the teams give feedback on each other's prototypes, at least three teams makes for a good interchange. If further people are available, the more the merrier! The DeepDive works well in teams of up to eight, and assuming you have the space and people power available, one facilitator should be able to handle up to four or five teams at once.

If you want to leverage the DeepDive in an even larger group, this is certainly possible – but you may then want to have more than one facilitator to make sure you have enough bandwidth to coach all the teams and help them to stay on track. We've had good experience with up to 80 participants, and up to ten or twelve parallel teams all DeepDiving at once, but it's best to try something smaller for your first time. In fact, a major technology firm is planning a DeepDive for over 300 participants in teams of 20 over one and a half days to help ensure the attendees exchange ideas and get real value from the expert speakers. The point is, the DeepDive is a flexible approach to effective teamwork across small to large numbers of professionals.

Sample DeepDive schedule

Step 1   Introduction: introduce the DeepDive process and the design challenge (60 minutes)

Step 2   Visiting the experts for ideas: cases, readings, role-playing, articles, videos, plus the experiences you bring with you. (Completed – we provided this preparation material, as there was no time allocated for it prior to the workshop) (15 minutes)

Step 3   First prototype design (including preliminary brainstorming) (60 minutes)

Step 4   First prototype provocation/frenzy (present, feedback, record – no debate!) (45 minutes)

Step 5   Second prototype design (including brainstorming) (45 minutes)

Step 6   Second prototype provocation/frenzy (30 minutes)

Step 7   Third prototype (including brainstorming) (45 minutes)

Step 8   Third prototype provocation/frenzy (30 minutes)

Step 9   Final design development and presentation (60 minutes)

Step 10   Discuss DeepDive process, results of prototyping, and general review and discussion (60 minutes)

Note: Bio breaks at some point: 10–15 minutes. Lunch. If we're lucky!

3. Create rapid prototypes: make sure your best ideas are real and substantive

Every DeepDive and, we believe, effective virtuoso teams in almost any setting, need to put ideas into play and test them as frequently as possible before the final results are committed to. The DeepDive forces teams to test their best ideas, by prototyping them as specific design solutions. Of course, for an issue of any complexity, a full solution probably represents a lot of work – perhaps days or even weeks. The purpose of the rapid prototyping phase is to very quickly try out the key elements of a design solution; in a sense to gain 'fast traction' on a problem. Focus on key elements only, not the entire solution with all the bells and whistles. With a prototype, use it to ask and answer the specific and vital few questions you want answered. There will be several prototypes in any

DeepDive, so you have lots of opportunities to ask different questions and get answers to different issues as the process evolves.

Many people have heard of prototyping before, from the worlds of information systems or product development, for example. In those contexts, a prototype is a way to quickly gain experience with key design issues, and to start getting customer feedback much earlier in the design cycle (without waiting for all the steps of the development process to have been completed). But prototyping doesn't have to be restricted to physical products. Rapid prototyping is *fully applicable* to any environment where a team needs to design a solution to a complex challenge. It can be applied to issues in marketing, organization design, strategy, and so on. This is a key conceptual point that you'll need to reinforce, because teams sometimes have a hard time believing that they can prototype anything other than physical products.

Why is prototyping powerful? Because your proposed solutions are put out in the open for everyone to react to and comment on. Prototypes should be seen as everyone's property. This is important in order to avoid the 'not invented here syndrome.' It also has other benefits; a prototype can create a vision of the future which is much more compelling than a mere plan or direction statement. Prototypes bring concepts to life, encouraging people to buy into a shared direction, and generating much more concrete and meaningful feedback at the early stages of a project than any other methodology we know. This is because a prototype is tangible – it's something you can easily discuss. Prototyping also reduces the risk inherent in creative processes – by trying out key elements of the solution before committing fully to its deployment. And because you're *rapidly prototyping* (that is, not building final products), there is little investment of time, money or ego. That makes it easy to rip apart a prototype and start from scratch, if a team discovers it is on the wrong track.

If prototyping magnifies the power of the design process, the DeepDive in turn magnifies the power of prototyping. It does this by compressing several cycles of prototyping into a short time period, thus accelerating your ability to try out key ideas and get feedback.

A good prototype is one which addresses the design challenge (or some key aspects of it), and which is as clear, tangible, and specific as possible. It can take almost any form – a prototype could be a storyboard on flipcharts, a model or framework, a process, a picture, an object, or even a skit where participants 'act out' key aspects of the solution. The important thing is that the prototype should be tangible enough to get across its key elements, and definite enough to get specific feedback during the next step. Each team needs to spend time at this step translating the key ideas from the brainstorming phase into some specific solution.

While the above guidelines are important, it's also key to *not* get too prescriptive or hung up on process at this point. The teams should feel empowered, especially during the first couple of prototyping sessions, to do original things in any way they think can capture the solution. That's why you've got toys and other supplies in the room. Encourage them to use these or any other ideas or materials they can think of. You may need to push them to be more aggressive or to fully pursue ideas to their conclusion.

It's important that the teams concentrate on what the prototype should be, rather than how to present or explain it – we believe that time spent on preparing PowerPoint presentations is time wasted at this stage, since you can and should expect prototypes to evolve radically over the course of the DeepDive, and the presentation creator is effectively absent from the team's conversation. Here are some tips the team have posted in team rooms, and on their individual DeepDive reminder cards:

RAPID PROTOTYPING TIPS

* Start with goal and intent – meet the design challenge

* Focus on high-risk areas

* Tailor prototype towards targeted questions

* Rough is good – no technique is too simple

* Try multiple approaches to the same issue

* Expect the unexpected

* Mix high-tech and low-tech components freely

* Build the prototypes fast and get direct feedback fast; learn!

* Use the prototype to get feedback, and move on

Source: IDEO

An important leadership task for this part of a DeepDive is to monitor each team's progress and to push them to get something *specific* completed during the limited time available. The time pressure serves to foster both teamwork (i.e. the team members work together against the clock, rather than worrying about the personal or organizational implications of the prototype) and prioritization (by giving time to work only on the most important parts of the prototype).

After the first prototyping phase, the teams need to get feedback on their initial solutions. There are a few ways to do this, which are discussed in the next section – the learning frenzy phase.

Important: Be aware that you will build several prototypes in a DeepDive and you will also frenzy and learn several times. The prototyping and frenzy steps form a powerful learning cycle that are repeated at least two and perhaps up to four times during a DeepDive that lasts, for ex-ample, one or two days.

4. Frenzy to test all prototypes: learning and feedback

At this step in the DeepDive, toward the end of the first solution cycle, the teams will have gathered information, brainstormed key elements of their solution, and built prototypes that capture and represent these key ideas. Now comes the moment of truth – or at least the moment of maximum learning. The teams will present their prototypes, get feedback, and take that feedback into the next prototyping cycle, so that the prototypes can be refined and improved.

There are many ways to get feedback. Late in the DeepDive, you may wish to have the teams present their prototypes to a panel of experts or to senior management, to help identify the key areas to focus on for the final design solution. However, to keep the energy level high and to enable the teams to learn from one another, at this stage teams should explain their prototype solutions to one another through a process that we call 'frenzy.'

The frenzy is a process where many teams explain their prototypes and get lots of feedback in parallel. It works especially well where the teams are grouped closely together – that's why you want one large room or adjacent rooms along a corridor. Each team keeps two of its members back in its own area, in order to explain their prototype solution to others, and sends the rest out to go look at the other teams' prototypes. Hence, if you have three teams of around six people, you will end up with six people staying with their own prototypes and the other twelve moving around and looking at all the rest.

Get everyone on their feet, both the presenters and reviewers should be moving around, and getting as much input as possible. The two presenters should work as a team, with one person explaining the prototype to the visitors and the other person capturing feedback. The presenter should show the prototype, and explain it *briefly*. This needs to be quick and to the point, and should be a description of the prototype rather than a discussion of how it was created or why it's great.

Next, the visitors provide feedback. The feedback, like the prototype description, must be fast and direct. You will need to watch the teams at this point, and provide some comments of your own to make sure that reviewers are blunt. Typical 'team' behaviors of saying lots of good things before critiquing, and being polite and sensitive when giving feedback, need to be set aside for this process to work. This doesn't mean that people should trash each other's work, but for this process to happen at the needed speed it must be very direct and honest. Since everyone is getting the same type of feedback at the same time, this is a fair approach. Anything less is wasting precious time.

Remember, your single most important role at this point is to encourage clear, honest, direct, and fast feedback. You should insist that everyone do this, and coach people to avoid excessive politeness and overly general or equivocal feedback. It is absolutely useless (at least for a DeepDive) to be told, for example: *'I think your prototype car is quite good . . . maybe it could use some more work, but I like it . . . I think I might drive it.'* It's much more valuable to be told: *'I like the front end a lot, but the tires will blow out in the first year on the road, and the tail lights are ugly.'* You will almost certainly need to coach and push the teams on this point, which means that you will need to sample the kinds of feedback people are giving to each prototype, and to move rapidly from team to team. You can be active in giving feedback as well, and your example can lay the groundwork for effective exchanges.

You will also need to coach prototype presenters on their reception of feedback. Especially if you've been successful in getting people to be honest and specific, it's natural for the teams who have worked hard on their prototypes to want to explain them more, or even to become defensive and start to argue with the person who's giving them feedback. This is bad for two reasons (at least): it will make the people giving feedback quickly revert to politeness and be less honest, and it will also reduce the amount of time spent listening (since someone who starts to explain or defend listens less effectively, and takes time which could be used for feedback).

To make a frenzy work, you need to set the right atmosphere. The purpose of the frenzy is not to evaluate the quality of the prototypes, nor to pick the best one, nor to debate whether a given concept is correct. At this early stage, every prototype will be full of holes, but may also have the essence of a great idea. The spirit should be: 'fail early and often to succeed sooner.' The more feedback, the better, because that can help to make the next prototype stronger and more complete.

You should emphasize these points both when introducing the DeepDive, and just before starting each of the frenzies, since people will tend to return to their normal 'polite' behaviors over time.

EVALUATION TIPS

* As a giver – ask direct and honest questions, give definite opinions, offer sincere suggestions

* As a giver – don't forget, what you see might be something you can use in your own prototype: 'steal with pride'

* As a receiver – don't justify or defend, accept gracefully
* As a receiver – remember to record so you don't lose track of suggestions
* As a receiver – try to overcome your biases for your own ideas: listen to what others have to say

The frenzy does not need to be long to be effective. Fifteen minutes may be enough for a good frenzy in a DeepDive of four to six teams, especially in the later rounds. The key is to give sufficient time for everyone to see all the prototypes, but only enough and no more. This is important, since in prototyping, imitation is the most sincere form of flattery. People who visit other teams should not only give feedback, but also capture the best of the other teams' ideas for future use by their own team – the 'steal with pride' idea.

Cycle back: The power of the DeepDive is driven by the continued iteration between prototyping and frenzying (challenging the prototype). This cycle drives experimenting and learning, towards a better and more effective solution.

Conclusion

If your teams need to be turbo-charged, consider thinking through a robust process that creates virtuoso team-like characteristics and capabilities. The DeepDive is one such process, and allows for teams across your organization to get tangible results, fast, within a set of constraints, utilizing the full potential of every team member.

A how-to guide

The previous sections have given you an overview of the DeepDive process. Next, we'll take you in great detail through the 12 steps of the DeepDive.

1 Define the design challenge

- *Make the design challenge clear, simple, and concise*
- *Include required output and timing*
- *Ask: how will a team know if a solution meets the objective?*
- *Make sure the challenge doesn't imply a solution*
- *Include constraints that ensure solutions are realistic and implementable, but try to avoid constraints that are at the cause of a problem (often these are organizational issues, which are self-inflicted and can be changed)*
- *'Test drive' the design challenge before the DeepDive*
- *You can choose a single design challenge for all sub-teams, or a different design challenge for each sub-team*

2 Build the team

- *Plan one or more dedicated blocks of time*
- *People are more important than timeline: adapt the timeline to get the right people*
- *Mix personalities – get enough 'ideas' people*
- *Maximize diversity – cultures, functions, roles, ages, insiders/outsiders*
- *Recruit experts – but not only experts! You also want people with no vested interest/no baggage*
- *Best to have around 12 to 30 people for your first DeepDive*

3 Get the room right

- *Pick an interesting and stimulating venue*
- *A large plenary area with space to move around*
- *Video and presentation support*
- *One room or area, with wall space, for each sub-team*
- *Sub-team rooms should be close together, or sections of the main room*
- *Set up rooms with inspirational posters and other visual materials*
- *Make prototyping materials accessible to all teams*

4 Set the stage – prep the teams, kick off the day

- *Build a tight, but realistic, agenda*
- *Make sure everyone understands the design challenge*
- *Name the teams*
- *Set the ground rules: follow the process, commit to the day*

- *Keep the pace rapid and the group together*
- *Don't make the agenda too rigid – allow for flexibility*

5 Visit the experts; learn, display, and share the issues

- *Consult some experts ahead of time, bring them to the DeepDive, or set aside time to visit them*
- *Share a 'starter set' of ideas and issues on the wall*
- *Have everyone visit the wall at the start of the DeepDive*
- *Mark the ideas that get used*
- *Re-visit the wall whenever inspiration is needed*

6 Brainstorm possible solutions to the design challenge

- *Review 'the rules' and insist they be followed*
- *It must be a team process – no individual listing of ideas*
- *Start with the best of the ideas from the wall of ideas*
- *Generate lots of ideas – go for quantity!*
- *Number the ideas*

7 Vote on the best solution ideas

- *Use silent voting or open voting to pick the best ideas for prototyping*
- *Be fast – first instincts can count*

8 Create rapid prototypes

- *Prototyping = learning*
- *Translate key ideas to tangible solutions*
- *Be bold and specific*
- *Trust the process*

- *Keep to the time deadlines*
- *No rules on format – there are many ways to prototype*

9 Frenzies – test prototypes and get rapid feedback

- *Two people per team present prototype and capture feedback*
- *Other members review and critique all the other prototypes*
- *Good feedback is blunt, honest, specific, and direct*
- *Those receiving feedback,* listen *and* record, *don't* defend
- *Move fast, keep the energy level high, and get a buzz going*

10 Repeat the cycle: brainstorm – prototype – frenzy

- *Minimum 3 cycles (including final) for ideas to develop*
- *Balance time between brainstorming, prototyping, and frenzies*
- *Push for* bold, aggressive *results*
- *Keep the energy high and the DeepDive moving*

11 Construct final prototype solution

- *Kick off the final prototype round by getting everyone together*
- *Allow a little more time for 'polishing'*
- *Motivate the teams – consider a contest or prize*
- *Each team should present their solution*
- *The teams should vote on best one, or best features of each*
- *Explain what happens next*

12 DeepDive review

- *On the spot, while the ideas are fresh*
- *Have each team come up with: what they would keep, what they would change, and what their recommendations for change are*
- *Your job is to listen and record, not to justify or defend*

Three examples of DeepDive agendas

A2

1. Product ideas DeepDive (10 teams, 60 people)

The design challenge

What are the top priority product ideas we should pursue in our research?

Schedule

60' **Set the stage**. Why are we here? Why do we need to generate new ideas? Explain key consumer benefits. Explanation of morning: logic, logistics, ground rules. Show DeepDive video.

60' **Visit the experts**. Teams discuss interesting ideas for new business. Look at ideas on wall generated before workshop (via e-mail) for inspiration. Choose your team's five best ideas and share them with the group. Each team puts flipchart page up in front of room. Each participant votes on what the most interesting ideas are (three votes each, but you can't vote on your own idea).

2.25 hours

2.75 hours

15' **Coffee break**. During break, facilitators aggregate the votes, and decide on the five ideas to be attacked after the break – our 'design challenge.'

10' **Regroup**: show the five ideas and explain next steps. One idea per table (and 2 tables per idea). Set expectations: '*Prototype solutions must be actions that you and your boss can track, monitor and discuss each time you meet.*'

   Set constraints: must meet at least one of the **key consumer benefits**, and **time-to-market must be less than 2 years**.

30' **Brainstorm** on the product idea assigned to you. How would it work? What technology does it require? Which key consumer benefits does it respond to? Who are the likely consumers?

20' **Prototype** a solution.

20' **First frenzy**. Share prototypes with other teams. Teams will split up; half of team stays at table, other half moves to visit two other teams at their tables to hear what they have come up with, and to offer comments/criticisms on their choices. No defending of prototypes, no long explanations – just listen and note criticisms/comments.

20' **Second prototype**. Take what we heard from the other teams, brainstorm what needs to be done, and then rework, improve and/or clarify our prototype.

20' **Second frenzy**, but this time it is a free-for-all, a marketplace of ideas. Grab anyone you can and explain your prototype and get feedback.

20' **Third and final prototype.**

20' All prototypes up on one wall or front of room. Everyone tours the wall. Look for commonalities, contradictions and early wins. Agree on what we don't agree on. Discuss next steps.

2.75 hours

2. Organization transformation DeepDive

The design challenge

Identify, for senior management consumption on Tuesday, the five top key success factors to ensure that the organization transformation on project X provides real, tangible value to your company by April 2xxx with noticeable progress and more value by July 2xxx.

Design constraints

1 You have to be able to present these five critical success factors (which are things that must be done right now, and done very well) to senior management by next Tuesday and the presentation can take no longer than 10 minutes.

2 The five critical success factors must drive the transformation you propose in a bold way.

3 The five critical success factors must be EBITDA (Earnings Before Interest, Taxes, Depreciation and Amortization) and customer value sensitive.

4 The five key success factors must be consistent with your company's objectives, values and brand promise.

Schedule

Teams already familiar with DeepDive, so no introduction needed.

Step 0:   Visiting the *experts* for ideas: cases, readings, role-playing, articles, videos, plus the experiences you bring with you. (Completed.)

Step 1:   First prototype design (including brainstorming) (45 minutes)

Step 2:   First prototype provocation (present, feedback, record) (30 minutes)

Step 3:   Second prototype design (including brainstorming) (45 minutes)

Step 4:   Second prototype provocation (30 minutes)

Step 5:   Third prototype (including brainstorming) (30 minutes)

Step 6:   Third prototype provocation (20 minutes)

Step 7:   Final design development (30 minutes)

Step 8:   Did we meet the design constraints? Will this design work? (30 minutes)

Step 9:   Discuss DeepDive process, results of prototyping, and general review and discussion (30 minutes)

Note: Bio breaks at some point: 10–15 minutes. Lunch. If we're lucky!

3. Process information DeepDive

Your design challenge

A **20-minute presentation** (maximum) by each team, which includes the following three key points:

1 **Describe the two key company processes you have been assigned.** What are they, how do they function and how do they link to or depend on the other processes? Be visual.

2 **Why are these processes important?** How are they linked to strategy?

3 **The elevator pitch.** Describe in 30 seconds the aspects of one or both of your group processes that are important for a new manager in the company.

Bonus: comments, critiques, suggestions, unanswered questions about your two processes, if you have any.

A few caveats:

▌ We are *not* asking you to create processes.

▌ We are *not* asking you to improve the processes.

▌ We are *not* asking you to critique the processes, but you can if you wish.

▌ Take each process 'as is', as you hear them from the specialists, and as you know them from your work.

Schedule

13:30 – 14:15 **Introduction to group processes session**
DeepDive video, schedule, rules, logistics.

14:15 – 14:45 Step 1: Team organization
Each team discusses amongst themselves their approach
to the assignment. Brainstorm and agree on strategy,
questions, definition and assignment of tasks. What
information do you need in order to complete the
assignment? Who will do what?

**14:45 – 15:15 Step 2: Group processes – 'learning from
the specialists'**
It is the responsibility of the participants to get this first
taste of each group process. Though you are focused on
two group processes for the assignment, you have to be
able to explain how your assigned processes link to the
others. Write down your ideas on something that you can
easily put up on to your wall later.

15:15 – 15:30 Break – put your collected ideas and
information on your team wall.

**15:30 – 16:00 Step 2 (continued): Group processes –
'Learning from the specialists' – the remaining processes**
Listen closely. Take notes. How do these processes link to
the three we heard earlier? What else do you want to know?

16:00 – 16:30 Step 3: Team
Regroup and share ideas. Put ideas on the team wall.
Look at everyone's inputs and then decide how to use the
next session. What is missing? What questions are not
yet answered?

**16:30 – 17:30 Step 4: 'Learning from the specialists' *in
detail***
One process specialist per room. Teams to choose which
specialists they visit and for how long.

17:30 – 18:15 **Step 5: Team – design first prototype of assignment**
Each team member must leave session with a prototype in their hands: *one sheet of paper that explains your prototype*. On a flipchart, list any un-answered questions you still have.

18:15 – end **Step 6: Share first prototypes with others**
during cocktails and stand-up dinner. What do they think? **Present your prototype** and **ask for feedback**, but **don't defend**, or go into long explanations, **just listen**. Write down the feedback.

08:30 – 09:30 **Step 7: Team – design second prototype**
What feedback did we get from users last night? What new ideas do we have? What did we learn from the prototypes of other groups? What didn't the users understand last night? What have we learned? Incorporate these ideas, suggestions and criticisms into your second prototype.

09:30 – 10:00 **Step 8: Test second prototype**
Split your team in half; one half stays at wall to explain to other teams. Other half visits another team. We'll do this twice. Home team gives quick presentation of their prototype (10 minutes max) and visiting team offers feedback.

Home team: Listen. Don't defend. Don't be afraid to 'fail.'

Visiting team: Be concise. Be helpful. Be honest.

10:00 – 10:45 **Step 9: Design final prototype**
Compare learning between prototypes. Complete your prototype.

10:45 – 11:00 **Break**

11:00 – 12:30 **Plenary discussion**

Presentation and discussion of each team's prototypes. Experts and senior management will be present to give feedback.

Sample of materials used in a DeepDive

TABLE 9.1 Material used for a DeepDive of 60 people (10 teams of 6)

Item	Number	Comments
Flipcharts	10	With tripod/stand
Pens	60	Normal pens
Markers	60	To write on flipcharts, various colors
Index cards	300	Size: at least 12 × 8 cm
Post-It notes	60	1 package per participant, various colors; at least 75 × 75 mm
Voting stickers	300	Round dots, bright colors, any size – they just need to be visual
Colored paper	180	Standard sheets (i.e. 8.5" × 11")
Scissors	10	One per team
Glue	10	Tube or stick
Tape	10	Scotch tape rolls
String	5	Balls
Aluminum foil	3	Normal kitchen rolls
Masking tape	10	Rolls
Exacto knife	10	
Cardboard	20	Standard sheets (i.e. A4 or 8.5" × 11")

You may want to provide materials that teams can, optionally, use to build their prototypes. It's up to you whether you want to do this – you can do successful DeepDives with or without these materials.

For the DeepDive example above, we provided the following in a central spot, easily accessible to all the teams. About half the teams made use of this option:

styrofoam sheets and blocks	plastic trays
corks	plastic bottles
curtain rod rings	plastic hooks
colored string	plastic tubing
steel washers, nuts, bolts	wooden popsicle sticks
wire	

Go to a do-it-yourself store or a hobby or craft shop, use your imagination, and remember, the teams will be using theirs as well. They're remarkably resourceful once they get going.

Index